THE POLITICS AND ETHICS OF REPRESENTATION IN QUALITATIVE RESEARCH

GH00730081

This book offers insights on politics and ethics of representation that are relevant to researchers concerned with struggles for justice. It takes moments of discomfort in the qualitative research process as important sites of knowledge for exploring representational practices in critical research.

The Politics and Ethics of Representation in Qualitative Research draws on experiences from research processes in nine PhD projects. In some chapters, ethical and political dilemmas related to representational practices are analyzed as experienced in fieldwork. In others, the focus is on the production of representation at the stage of writing. The book deals with questions such as: What does it mean to write about the lives of others? How are ethics and politics of representation intertwined, and how are they distinct? How are politics of representation linked to a practice of solidarity in research? What are the im/possibilities of hope and care in research?

Drawing on grounded empirical research, the book offers input to students, PhDs, researchers, practitioners, activists and others dealing with methodological dilemmas from a critical perspective. Instead of ignoring discomforts, or describing them as solved, we stay with them, showing how such a reflective process provides new, ongoing insights.

The Critical Methodologies Collective consists of nine feminist researchers early in their careers with a shared interest in, and discomfort of, doing critical research. The members come from varied social, political and academic backgrounds, with roots and routes in Denmark, Finland, India, Iran, Poland, Sweden, Turkey and the UK.

THE POLITICS AND ETHICS OF REPRESENTATION IN QUALITATIVE RESEARCH

Addressing Moments of Discomfort

Edited by The Critical Methodologies Collective

Routledge
Taylor & Francis Group

LONDON AND NEW YORK

First published 2022
by Routledge
2 Park Square, Milton Park, Abingdon, Oxon OX14 4RN

and by Routledge
605 Third Avenue, New York, NY 10158

Routledge is an imprint of the Taylor & Francis Group, an informa business

Illustrations by Sarah Katarina Hirani

British Library Cataloguing-in-Publication Data
A catalogue record for this book is available from the British Library

Library of Congress Cataloging-in-Publication Data
Names: Critical Methodologies Collective, editor.
Title: The politics and ethics of representation in qualitative research : addressing moments of discomfort / edited by The Critical Methodologies Collective.
Identifiers: LCCN 2021002951 (print) | LCCN 2021002952 (ebook) | ISBN 9780367281014 (hardback) | ISBN 9780367281038 (paperback) | ISBN 9780429299674 (ebook)
Subjects: LCSH: Qualitative research. | Research--Political aspects. | Research--Moral and ethical aspects.
Classification: LCC H62 .P615 2021 (print) | LCC H62 (ebook) | DDC 174/.900142--dc23
LC record available at https://lccn.loc.gov/2021002951
LC ebook record available at https://lccn.loc.gov/2021002952

ISBN: 978-0-367-28101-4 (hbk)
ISBN: 978-0-367-28103-8 (pbk)
ISBN: 978-0-429-29967-4 (ebk)

Typeset in Bembo
by SPi Global, India

CONTENTS

PREFACE

We are a collective of feminist researchers early in their careers. We come from varied social, political and academic backgrounds, with roots and routes in Denmark, Finland, India, Iran, Poland, Sweden, Turkey and the UK. Although we denominated our group the Critical Methodologies Collective only a few years ago, we have been meeting regularly since 2012. This book – which draws on experiences from research processes in our nine PhD projects to engage with issues of ethics and politics of representation – originates from those gatherings. Therefore, we want to begin by telling our story of becoming a collective. Like other stories of becoming, ours is neither linear nor complete. Time is central to writing – we write about the past, with and against time in the present, hoping that the writing will advance an intellectual endeavour in the future.

It all started with a critical methodology workshop moderated by Yasmin Gunaratnam at Lund University, Sweden. The workshop brought together doctoral students in social sciences to discuss methodological issues in their research. Some of the authors in this volume were among those lucky students. Working with Yasmin Gunaratnam was a transformative experience. During the workshop, Yasmin provided us not only with critical feedback on our research projects but also with tools to realize and situate commonalities and differences in our research ideals, methodological anxieties and academic vulnerabilities in relation to multiple relations of power and inequality. Yasmin's nurturing pedagogy encouraged us to organize a critical methodologies group.

We started as a small working group of doctoral students. Initially, we read and discussed texts from queer, feminist, materialist and decolonial/postcolonial scholars which we considered significant in order to situate, problematize and liberate our research practices and discomforts. As the politics of the group began solidifying and our PhD projects progressed, we began discussing our work-in-progress in the group meetings. Trying to resist ideals imposed by the neoliberal academy, which measure progress by the quantity of produced texts, one of our commitments has become to imbibe the reflexive practice to 'count what others don't' (Mountz *et al.* 2015, p. 1250).

An important point in our history was another methodology workshop we arranged, this time with Les Back. The workshop inspired us to think of writing collectively on the challenges we faced and the solidarities we built while conducting research as doctoral students. It would take a few more years to materialize our thoughts. This book grew from that idea.

∧ ↓ ∠

Working on this book has involved collective writing days, workshops with scholars who inspire us – Bridget Anderson, Diana Mulinari, Johanna Esseveld and Yasmin Gunaratnam – and a joint editorial process over a period of time that was probably longer than is usual for edited volumes and called for a very close collaboration.

Signing the agreement with the publisher opened up for questions that forced us to reflect on how we wanted to work on the volume: How would we resolve the editorship with this many involved members? Who should stand as editors? And how could the ideals of working as a collective be translated into the legal language of copyrights and liabilities? We decided that we wanted the Collective to stand as editor and author of some parts of the book, and came up with a solution that made it formally possible: we registered the Collective as a legal association. This process helped us to articulate what was important for the group and what visions we had in terms of collective writing. But it also showed that going against what is the norm in academic work requires extra labour and inventiveness.

A practice of care has been central to the Collective, especially because, by deciding to work on moments of discomfort in our research, we opened up a space in which we allowed ourselves to become vulnerable. One very crucial common denominator permeating the work process has been the unease in writing about these matters. After all, we were not only sharing our experiences during the work of our PhD theses; we were likewise revisiting our emotions. Writing about it was, for all of us to different extents, also associated with a degree of discomfort. We have learned through the process of writing this book (and with the help of scholars such as Anzaldúa 2002 and hooks 1994) that creating and working to obtain a space where we can present ourselves and our ideas is not necessarily a friction-free course of action. Our work process, and the formation of a collective, have, similar to the experience described by Gannon *et al.* (2016), proven to be more than a process of connecting us with one another. We do not share the same experiences of class, employment status, sexuality, gender, racialization and citizenship status, and, as such, not all of our political and theoretical knowledge has been elaborated in our joint work. Acknowledging our differences, we see the collective work over the last couple of years, and especially in the labour of this book, as a space where we have been allowed to test ideas and 'bridge' (Anzaldúa 2002) some of the differences between us. For us, it is important to stress this loosening of our borders and to emphasize: We are not 'one' but we form a collective.

The Critical Methodologies Collective

References

Anzaldúa, G., 2002. Preface. (Un)natural bridges, (Un)safe spaces. In: G. Anzaldúa and A. Keating, eds. *This bridge we call home: radical visions for transformation*. New York: Routledge, 1–5.

Gannon, S. et al., 2016. Uneven Relationalities, Collective Biography, and Sisterly Affect in Neoliberal Universities. *Feminist Formations*, 27 (3), 189–216. doi:10.1353/ff.2016.0007.

hooks, b., 1994. *Teaching to Transgress: Education as the Practice of Freedom*. New York: Routledge.

Mountz, A. et al., 2015. For slow scholarship: A feminist politics of resistance through collective action in the Neoliberal University. *Acme: An International E-Journal for Critical Geographies*, 14 (4), 1235–1259.

ACKNOWLEDGEMENTS

This volume is the result of a long timeframe of labour by the Collective. Within that timeframe, numerous individuals and institutions have helped us shape the insights presented in this book, to develop and sustain a commitment to a collective thinking and writing practice. Their encouragement, caring acts, words of kindness and their support also helped us not to fall apart or get stuck throughout the process.

First and foremost, we express our deepest gratitude to the many individuals across many countries who as research participants, interlocutors and comrades have made all of our scholarship possible. They, unfortunately, must remain anonymous, but they know who they are. We remain deeply grateful for their engagement, conversations, trust, rapport, care and inspiration, even amidst precarious conditions. This book could not have been written without them.

We are deeply indebted to Bridget Anderson, Les Back, Johanna Esseveld, Yasmin Gunaratnam and Diana Mulinari, who read and commented on both earlier and final drafts of the manuscript. This book would not have been achieved without their workshops, critical reading, intellectual reserves, scholarly commitment and support. Their scholarship is truly transformative and we have un/learned a lot from them. Perhaps the only way to repay our debt is to practise what we have learned from them about critical methodologies, engaged pedagogy, political labour, hope and solidarity.

We acknowledge and appreciate all who participated in the Collective's ongoing process of becoming, in various ways and at different stages. Their insights are embedded into this volume. Special thanks to Ina Knobblock, Ann Kristin Lassen, Kristin Linderoth and Maria Tonini for their generous sharing of ideas, emotions, experiences, questions and answers. We also express our gratitude to the many friends, colleagues and mentors who read various parts of our draft chapters at different points in time. It is also through their efforts that this volume has been possible.

Several institutions supported our collaboration. Our universities and departments provided funding for workshops, conference participation, and editorial and artistic work, all of which enabled and enhanced this project. Many thanks to: the Department of Gender Studies, the Department of Psychology, the Department of Social Work and the Department of Sociology, at the Faculty of Social Sciences at Lund University; and the Department of Social Work at Malmö University. Lund University's open-access book publishing fund enabled us to materialize our political commitment to attain accessible research and knowledge. We hope that, in the very near future, all barriers that make knowledge difficult to access will be demolished and there will be no need to apply for grants to make it more accessible.

Last but not least, we would like to thank Lucy Edyvean for her meticulous work. Lucy is a copy editor who not only takes care of the text but also the author. We truly appreciate her caring editing style, and fabulous and uplifting emails. We would also like to acknowledge the artistic labour of Sarah Katarina Hirani. Sarah is an illustrator whose imagination and ability to create images from the written word are truly impressive. Our gratitude also goes to Hannah Shakespeare at Routledge, who assisted us throughout the process.

CONTRIBUTORS

Pankhuri Agarwal School of Sociology, Politics and International Studies, University of Bristol, Bristol, UK

Pouran Djampour Division of Migration, Ethnicity and Society (REMESO), Linköping University, Sweden

Eda Hatice Farsakoglu Department of Sociology, Lund University, Sweden

Marta Kolankiewicz Department of Gender Studies, Lund University, Sweden

Tove Lundberg Department of Psychology, Lund University, Sweden

Diana Mulinari Department of Gender Studies, Lund University, Sweden

Vanna Nordling Department of Social Work, Malmö University, Sweden

Katrine Scott Department of Social Education, University College Copenhagen, Denmark

Johanna Sixtensson Department of Social Work, Malmö University, Sweden

Emma Söderman School of Social Work, Lund University, Sweden

INTRODUCTION

The Critical Methodologies Collective

In qualitative research, the research process is often filled with moments of discomfort. These discomforts can appear at any stage of the research: when choosing the subject of research, during fieldwork, in the process of analysis and when presenting research findings to different audiences. In this edited volume, we take these moments of discomfort seriously and use them as sites of knowledge production for reflecting on the politics and ethics of the qualitative research process. By locating our experiences in implementing nine different PhD projects carried out in different disciplines and research contexts in social sciences, we argue that these moments of discomfort help us to gain important insights into the methodological, theoretical, ethical and political issues that are crucial for the fields we engage with. Drawing on feminist and other critical discussions (Mulinari and Sandell 1999, Gunaratnam 2003, Back 2007, Gunaratnam and Hamilton 2017), we deal with questions such as: What does it mean to write about the lives of others? What are the ethical modes and conundrums of producing representations? In research projects that are located in the tradition of critical or engaged scholarship, how are ethics and politics of representation intertwined, and when are they distinct? How are politics of representation linked to the practice of solidarity in research? What are the im/possibilities of hope and care in research?

Representation, solidarity and accountability in qualitative research

Qualitative research is a representational practice, in the sense that it is concerned with making sense of the world, by understanding and interpreting the meanings of different practices, phenomena and processes. This is done by constructing representations of those who are being analyzed. Representational practices in research, like any other representational practices, always involve a process of translation (Hall 1997). Such a process carries in it an inherent violence of transformation, reduction or obliteration (cf. Hastrup 1992). In this sense, it opens up space for dilemmas of ethics of representation. Such general questions of research ethics should, however, not be divorced from questions concerning research politics. As we have learned from conceptualizations of, as well as debates on, the working of representation in feminist, critical and post-colonial fields (Foucault 1970[2002], Said 1978[2003], Hall 1997, hooks 1999, Ahmed 2000), these processes are not innocent, but deeply implicated in power relations of societies that the research concerns. In this sense, to create a representation is always a political endeavour. It is also the case in critical research that aims at producing knowledge that is concerned with issues of justice. While structuralist and semiotic traditions teach us how representational practices operate, critical, feminist and post-colonial traditions encourage us to contextualize these practices in particular historical moments in order to explore their implications for imposing and maintaining, but also resisting, unjust social structures.

A basic condition in qualitative research is that it is impossible as a researcher to fully understand every aspect of people or communities we conduct research with, with the resultant conundrum in representation. It is impossible to acquire 'full representation on the one hand, and full comprehension on the other', which can be seen as an inherent failure (Visweswaran 1994, p. 100). This inherent failure should be recognized by the researcher, something that would allow to 'question the authority of the investigating subject without paralyzing him' (Spivak 1998, p. 276). This means carefully reflecting on the practice of creating representations of other people, while not letting these critical reflections lead to a state of not being able to do any representations at all.

In this volume, politics and ethics of representational practices in research are considered in relation to the question of accountability. Based on Haraway's discussions of accountability as part of feminist objectivity, Bhavnani (1993) holds that anyone who claims to undertake feminist research must carefully avoid reproducing dominant representations which reinforce inequality. Accountability, then, she argues, is both about being accountable towards individuals (research subjects) as well as being accountable to the 'overall project of feminism' (1993, p. 98). In many of the research projects discussed in this book, this question is complicated by the fact that researchers often face competing or even conflicting accountabilities. Most importantly, tensions might occur between accountability towards the research participants and accountability towards political struggles in which the research project is situated (see the chapter by Tove Lundberg and the chapter by Vanna Nordling in this volume). Some key questions that we pose to ourselves in this context are: What modes of representation are both ethically accountable to those represented in the study *and* politically accountable in the context of contentious justice struggles? And what if these two types of accountabilities not only diverge, but even remain in tension? It is when asking these questions that we might find it productive to distinguish between the ethics and the politics of research. All our studies are politically committed to different struggles of social justice: from queer recognition of non-binary sex characteristics, through asylum rights and migrants' rights, to antiracist critique, we recognize and adhere to a particular ideal of knowledge production in academia – one that understands the role and significance of social science in reproducing, supporting and opposing power structures.

This type of critical research often builds on an epistemology where partial perspectives coming from 'below' are seen to have the potential of creating more valid situated knowledges, as these positions will render visible the structures of power in our society, as well as structures present in the production of knowledge (Haraway 1988; also see Harding 2004, p. 128). Importantly, these positions at the margin, creating partial perspectives from below, are not static or universal. Oppression is produced through social relations and played out differently in regard to time and context (Mohanty 1988). The positions of social movements with which researchers claim to stand in solidarity, as well as the positions of researchers, need to be subjected to a thorough reflexive engagement (Harding 2004). Simultaneously, the knowledge produced by and in collaboration with social movements should be acknowledged as creating relevant and grounded analyses (Mulinari and Sandell 1999). Striving to research in solidarity brings to the fore a range of ethical as well as political challenges. Scholars who have worked in sensitive and precarious settings often emphasize the importance of recognizing challenges of asymmetric power relations, representation, trust and suspicion, risks, agency and human rights (Mackenzie *et al.* 2007). An important aspect of this is that the precarious situation for people and/or communities who have been subject to research has led researchers to conclude that we must formulate research projects that contribute something back to the communities and individuals, and that research participants need to be involved in the production of research (Huisman 2008, Düvell *et al.* 2010). These are examples where the ethical dilemmas related to power asymmetries also led to researchers formulating and carrying out their research in modified ways. Although these are honourable ambitions of handling power asymmetries in a constructive way, it does diminish the fact that researchers gain academically from the interaction, whilst the benefits for the participants might be less clear (Sinha and Back 2014; see discussion in Pankhuri Agarwal's chapter in this volume).

Solidarity in a context of critical research can hence be actualized in the meeting between the researchers and the subjects of the enquiry: what can a solidary position as a researcher entail within a relation many times characterized by power asymmetries? What stories are we to tell, how do we tell them, and how to 'get hold of them'? Matters of accountability and representation are hence brought (back) to the fore. We do not claim to 'solve' these issues – doing research in solidarity with movements and struggles will always bring about tensions and ambivalence – but we find it crucial to address and scrutinize them to bring to light how to address, engage with and embrace the discomforts in each case of research.

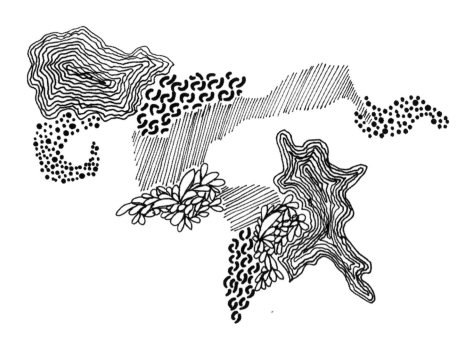

Overview of the book

The chapters that make up this volume draw on experiences from research processes in nine projects. They all engage with issues of ethics and politics of representation in different ways. In some chapters, ethical and political dilemmas related to representational practices are analyzed as experienced in the fieldwork. In others, the focus is on production of representation at the stage of writing the text. Still others draw parallels between these stages. While the moments of discomfort that open up for different dilemmas are specific to the particular research process, we hope that they will resonate with similar dilemmas in other fields and contexts as well as disciplines.

In a dialogical piece opening this volume, Tove Lundberg captures how the choice of terms and definitions – both in conversations with the research participants and in the text produced by the researcher – might entail politically infected dilemmas that go beyond conceptualization of the object of her study. She articulates how, in the research project on variations in sex characteristics, usually referred to as 'intersex' or 'disorders of sex development', she was struggling when choosing how to talk about her research and address her participants. Lundberg shows how this choice had to do with particular politics of representation and how using certain terminology not only entailed a commitment to a particular scientific explanation of the phenomenon she was studying, but also situated her work politically in relation to different justice struggles. Lundberg shows how this dilemma reflected something at the very core of her study: the ways in which sex characteristics are constructed in a binary system where there are clear options and no in-betweens allowed, and explores whether it is possible to navigate in less categorical ways the conceptual, theoretical and political choices she has been confronted with.

The issue of ethics of representation arises at the very beginning of the fieldwork, by being related to living up to such central ethical requirements as informed consent. When we engage with other people's lives with an aim of producing a representation of them, how can we be sure that those represented consent to this? Johanna Sixtensson describes in her chapter how giving consent or 'saying no' to being represented in a research project is a complicated practice that should not be reduced to a single act or signature on an official consent form. Her account of an exchange with one of her young research participants, both at the time of the fieldwork and after her thesis had been published, discloses complexities and ambivalences of asking for and giving consent.

In another way, the issues of representation are at the heart of Emma Söderman's chapter. Söderman explores the work around the *No Border Musical*, in which she herself performed. In her thesis, she analyzes not only the ways in which a representation of the experience of borders was created in the musical by a group of activists that included irregular migrants, but also how working on the musical opened up for practices of commoning. There are two levels of representational practice in her work: the theatrical representation of the musical and the representation produced as a result of research. In her chapter, Söderman explores what we as researchers can learn about representation from the method of community theatre, in which people with and without the experience of irregular migration work together. She shows how on the stage irregular migrants are confronted by what she conceptualizes as *faceness* – an expectation of embodying the representation of the other. Söderman's chapter illustrates how issues of aesthetic representation – be it through performative arts or in text – are closely related to issues of representation in the political sense of the term. The question thus is not only where the source of frames of reference for representation is located, but also who is expected to represent or stand for the other.

A commonality of experiences in the field – and more exactly of the experience of waiting – is used as a point of departure in the chapter by Pankhuri Agarwal. Describing her fieldwork in the research on internal migrant workers in Delhi, who are struggling for their rights through legal proceedings, she shows how her waiting in the field became a site of knowledge in itself. By waiting for some research participants and waiting together with others, she learns not only about the workings of legal institutions in India, but also about how particular hierarchies and power relations are produced through temporal and spatial aspects of waiting. While experiencing waiting, with all its frustration and discomfort, which becomes for Agarwal a methodological tool in itself and a way of connecting with her research participants, she also shows how her experience of waiting is fundamentally different from that of the workers'. In a way, the very act of representing the experience of waiting transforms this experience and thereby creates a distance from the participants, suggesting the limits of commonality in the field.

In yet another way, the issues of representation – both in the field and in text – are present in the chapter by Katrine Scott. In ethnographic work, being in the field also involves a self-representational practice, when the ethnographer represents themselves to the research participants. Scott describes her search for finding a common ground with university students in Iraqi Kurdistan. She explores her performance of middle-class respectability in the field using concepts of 'studying sideways' and 'matching' and shows how these strategies open up for certain possibilities, while at the same time they bear risks of obliterating differences and power relations in the research process. In the second part of her chapter, Scott illustrates how the question of self-representation is not limited to the fieldwork, but continues in the process of writing: she explains how she used auto-ethnographic accounts as entry points to analysis, and discusses what such a stylistic choice means for representational practice of the other in relation to the ethnographic self.

Another contribution, written by Vanna Nordling, deals with the politics of representation in relation to expectations of inscribing one's research into a particular field. In her chapter, Nordling analyzes the dilemma of representing her research on social workers supporting migrants whose application for asylum has been rejected. She writes about how her framing of the topic would shift when presenting to different audiences, in different research fields and in a changing political climate: making visible diverse, often conflicting, expectations of how social workers should be portrayed and their practices understood. In a way, the chapter illustrates how representation created in the research is always a product of available frames co-created by other scholars, disciplines, institutions and political contexts in which the research is produced. Nordling's chapter, in a somewhat similar way to Söderman's, touches upon the issue of visibility of representation and its use for the political struggles, when such visibility might actually transpire to carry very concrete risks.

Another chapter addressing issues of representation in relation to the writing process is by Marta Kolankiewicz. It describes the process of anonymization in research on anti-Muslim racism in courts of law in Sweden. Kolankiewicz explores representational practices in relation to the significance of proper names of those depicted in the research. She analyzes the working of different anonymization procedures – from erasing original names, through substituting them by numbers or symbols, to giving pseudonyms – in order to ask questions about the politics and ethics of such operations. By situating these practices in the context of research on racism, Kolankiewicz shows how names are significant markers of difference in racist discourses and practices, but at the same time meaningful signs that carry with them diverse histories of racialization that should not be obliterated if we want to understand different experiences of racism. Finally, she poses the question of the role of the proper name for the possibility of attending to the singularity of the stories represented in the research.

The final chapter builds on a conversation between Pouran Djampour and Eda Hatice Farsakoglu and deals with the practice of care in the field and in research more broadly. Djampour and Farsakoglu set out from their observations from doing research with young people with experience of migrating to Sweden and with Iranian LGBTQ refugees in Turkey waiting for resettlement to a third country, respectively. They analyze caring encounters in the field through a reflexive lens. They argue that creating knowledge together with, and learning from, research participants involves making oneself vulnerable. They also show how caring encounters and relationships between researcher and research participants may alter both the research process and the content of ethnographic material, with an awareness of the challenges, limitations, multiplicities and contradictions inherent in ethnographic research. Djampour and Farsakoglu close the chapter by addressing the reader and proposing that the practice of *sharing* – a practice that started through the given encounters with the research participants – instantiates the practice of *care* itself. In a way, this final point relates to all the chapters of this volume, which have been written with the intention of sharing moments of discomfort.

References

Ahmed, S., 2000. *Strange Encounters: Embodied Others in Post-Coloniality*. London; New York: Routledge.

Back, L., 2007. *The Art of Listening*. London and New York: Bloomsbury.

Bhavnani, K.-K., 1993. Tracing the Contours: Feminist Research and Feminist Objectivity. *Women's Studies International Forum*, 16 (2), 95–104.

Düvell, F., Triandafyllidou, A. and Vollmer, B. 2010. Ethical Issues in Irregular Migration Research in Europe. *Population, Space and Place*, 16 (3), 227–239.

Foucault, M. (1970 [2002]). *The Order of Things: An archaeology of the human sciences*. Routledge.

Gunaratnam, Y., 2003. *Researching Race and Ethnicity: Methods, Knowledge and Power*. London: SAGE. ISBN 978-0761972877.

Gunaratnam, Y. and Hamilton, C., 2017. Introduction: The Wherewithal of Feminist Methods. *Feminist Review*, 115 (1), 1–12. ISSN 0141-7789.

Hall, S., ed., 1997. *Representation: Cultural Representation and Signifying Practices*. London; California; New Delhi: SAGE.

Haraway, D., 1988. Situated Knowledges: The Science Question in Feminism and the Privilege of Partial Perspective. *Feminist Studies*, 14 (3), 575–599.

Harding, S., 2004. Rethinking Standpoint Epistemology: What Is 'Strong Objectivity'? In: Sandra Harding, ed. *The Feminist Standpoint Theory Reader*. London: Routledge.

Hastrup, K., 1992. Out of Anthropology: The Anthropologist as an Object of Dramatic Representation. *Cultural Anthropology*, 7 (3), 327–345.

hooks, b., 1999. *Wounds of Passion: A Writing Life*. New York: Holt Paperbacks.

Huisman, K., 2008. 'Does This Mean You're Not Going to Come Visit Me Anymore?': An Inquiry into an Ethics of Reciprocity and Positionality in Feminist Ethnographic Research. *Sociological Inquiry*, 78 (3), 372–396.

Mackenzie, C., McDowell, C. and Pittaway, E., 2007. Beyond 'Do No Harm': The Challenge of Constructing Ethical Relationships in Refugee Research. *Journal of Refugee Studies*, 20 (2), 299–319.

Mohanty, C., 1988. Under Western Eyes: Feminist Scholarship and Colonial Discourses. *Feminist Review*, 30, 61–88.

Mulinari, D. and Sandell, K., 1999. Exploring the Notion of Experience in Feminist Thought. *Acta Sociologica*, 42 (4), 287–297.

Said, E.W. (1978 [2003]). *Orientalism*. Penguin.

Sinha, S. and Back, L., 2014. Making Methods Sociable: Dialogue, Ethics and Authorship in Qualitative Research. *Qualitative Research*, 14 (4), 473–487. ISSN 1468-7941.

Spivak, G., 1998. *In other Worlds: Essays in Cultural Politics*. New York: Routledge.

Visweswaran, K., 1994. *Fictions of Feminist Ethnography*. Minneapolis, MN; London: University of Minnesota Press.

1

BECOMING 'UNSTUCK' AMONG POSITIONALITIES, TERMS AND DISCIPLINES VIA CONVERSATION (WITH MYSELF)

Exploring Potentials for Affective Reflexivity in Critical Intersex Studies

Tove Lundberg

> In memory […] there's no ahead and no behind really, is there? Memory wells up in the now, in vertical time. And remembered time, as you know, is shot through with imagination.

(Hustvedt, 2019)

RESEARCHER TOVE: So, where do I start to write reflexively?

CLINICAL PSYCHOLOGIST TOVE: Well, I guess I am stating the obvious now, but I think you just did.

RESEARCHER: I guess I did. By conversing with an externalized part of myself, which is you. Just as if I were doing a Gestalt therapy exercise?

CLINICAL PSYCHOLOGIST: Yes, you have split off a part of yourself in order to experience yourself more clearly from different perspectives, just like in Gestalt therapy.

RESEARCHER: Great. I guess the next reasonable question to answer is why we are here.

CLINICAL PSYCHOLOGIST: Well, yes, I was just about to ask.

RESEARCHER: Sure. Okay, let's see how to articulate that. {*Thinking*} Well, before I became a researcher, I worked as a clinical psychologist for several years.

CLINICAL PSYCHOLOGIST: Mm-hmm.

RESEARCHER: As a clinical psychologist, you are such an important part of me and inform my thinking. However, you are never explicitly acknowledged in my academic work. I often feel like I have to choose a certain role or positionality in representing myself in academia, which usually excludes you. I was wondering if this kind of conversation would help me acknowledge the 'in-between-ness' of us that I feel that I embody.

CLINICAL PSYCHOLOGIST: Okay.

RESEARCHER: And as a PhD candidate, I didn't really explicitly talk to others about how to navigate the complexity of positions, roles, stakes, interests, feelings and so on that I guess most researchers experience.

CLINICAL PSYCHOLOGIST: So, instead you converse with yourself.

RESEARCHER: Yes, I guess so. {Laughs}

CLINICAL PSYCHOLOGIST: Well, as a clinical psychologist, I think that talking about things, even with yourself, is usually better than being silent about it. So what will be the topic for our current conversation?

RESEARCHER: You know my doctoral research on variations in sex characteristics (see Lundberg 2017).[1]

CLINICAL PSYCHOLOGIST: Yes, I know. What about it?

RESEARCHER: Well, I have this feeling of discomfort, which haunts me. That I wasn't reflexive enough during my doctoral research. I mean, I didn't write anything about reflexivity in my thesis and I just can't let that go. I feel like a bad qualitative researcher.

CLINICAL PSYCHOLOGIST: Okay, so do you mean that not including reflexive sections explicitly in your thesis suggests that you were not reflexive at all during your PhD project?

RESEARCHER: Well, drawing on ideas by scholars such as Skeggs (2002), I think I was doing some kind of reflexivity even though I didn't make my reflexive self explicit in the text? Today, I am quite inspired by Alvesson's and Sköldberg's (2017) idea of reflexivity as happening when 'thinking is confronted with another way of thinking' (p. 384) – that reflexivity can be about challenging our *thinking*. And I think I was doing that. However, the research process just felt like a mess and, by the end of it, I was just so happy to have a thesis to hand in at all.

CLINICAL PSYCHOLOGIST: So, by challenging your thinking, one interpretation is that you actively reflected during your research at least?

RESEARCHER: Maybe. I guess I was doing 'reflection-in-action', to borrow Schön's (1995) words. Schön's thinking informed the way I reflected on my practice as a clinical psychologist. I guess I just used what I had and went with it? However, I feel that this reflexive practice could have been more theoretically informed; that I should have 'grounded' myself in a reflexive perspective earlier.

CLINICAL PSYCHOLOGIST: Yes, well, that is always part of a process, isn't it? That you are where you are and it is hard to be somewhere else, especially to be more knowledgeable than you are?

RESEARCHER: Yes, I guess so. That is also why I chose to be part of writing this book. I want to use this space to look at my 'reflexivity in retrospect', as Doucet and Mauthner (2007) call it, as a form of what Schön (1995) describes as 'reflection-on-action'. In what way did I actually practise reflexivity? What kinds of ideas and theories was I drawing on that were behind the scenes and not really made explicit in my thesis? And did my practices of reflexivity actually make my research any better (Pillow 2003)?

CLINICAL PSYCHOLOGIST: That makes sense. And you want to explore this with me?

RESEARCHER: Yes, I want to explore it with you. Because I understand, now, that your perspectives and ideas were crucial in how the thesis developed. However, I never explicitly acknowledged in the text the expertise you brought to the thesis. Perhaps because it was so subconscious and unarticulated even within myself? And because I didn't utilize your knowing systematically? So, this chapter is a way of making sense of what I was doing as a PhD candidate and trying to make your input more explicit and transparent.

CLINICAL PSYCHOLOGIST: That sounds reasonable.

RESEARCHER: I also think that this has more general implications as well, because I am starting to understand how a dialogue between qualitative methodology and clinical psychology, in a broad perspective, can be very constructive. I think we need more texts that acknowledge these kinds of conversations. And maybe this text can contribute to the small body of literature that does exactly that as well as open up for other collective and interdisciplinary conversations where research positionalities and perspectives can be highlighted in constructive ways (see e.g. Hollway and Jefferson 2011)?

CLINICAL PSYCHOLOGIST: That sounds reasonable. So, how do we move on in this conversation to be able to attend to what is important?

RESEARCHER: Well, I thought that in the next section we would try to reconstruct some of our conversations from 2012 and onwards.[2] I was really struggling with terminology during my PhD project, and your input helped me move forward when I felt stuck. I thought we could focus on that. And then, I thought, we could end this chapter with a reflection on what happened during my PhD project.

CLINICAL PSYCHOLOGIST: Sounds like an interesting exploration. Let's travel back in time, then, to 2012 when you'd just started your PhD position.

Reconstructing my discomfort with terminology[3] as a PhD candidate in 2012 and onwards

RESEARCHER TOVE: {*Clearly frustrated*} Okay, so here's the thing. What should I even write in the material I use to recruit participants? Should I use, or should I avoid, terms such as 'intersex' and 'disorders of sex development' (DSD)? I just feel so frustrated. And whatever term I use, I will position myself in the topic area as either from the human rights or the medical perspective, in a way that I feel uncomfortable with. I also feel that whatever term I use I will offend some people. I really feel stuck!

CLINICAL PSYCHOLOGIST TOVE: Well, what did you write in the things you sent to the ethical review boards in Sweden and the UK before you started your project?

RESEARCHER: That this is research {*reads from information sheet*} 'about young people whose sex development has been different from others: they may have been different from birth, or they may have become different at some time in their development'.

CLINICAL PSYCHOLOGIST: Well, perhaps use that?

RESEARCHER: {*Stirred up*} Sure, but how do I WRITE about it? I can't write that in every sentence in my thesis! I need a noun, a term, something to represent the phenomena I am supposed to explore! Should I perhaps find language that works irrespective of perspective, that would be as descriptive as possible? 'Atypical sex development'?

CLINICAL PSYCHOLOGIST: Hmm… Just thinking critically here… Do you really think that 'atypical sex development' is *more descriptive* than 'intersex' or 'disorders of sex development'?

RESEARCHER: No, I guess not. That's actually also kind of normative. And also, if I use yet another term, I will perhaps neither be able to stay in conversations with those communities who use 'intersex', nor those who use 'DSD'. So what should I do?

CLINICAL PSYCHOLOGIST: {*Thinking*} Well, do you really need to figure it out now? And are you sure that you, of all people, are the one who should be sitting here in your room and trying to figure this out on your own? You are more than one year into your PhD project and you really need to start doing interviews as soon as you have ethical permissions. Perhaps you just have to throw yourself out there and see what happens? Perhaps the answers you are looking for are not in your head but could be articulated in conversations with the people who live these experiences in their everyday lives?

RESEARCHER: Good point. That feels like the first thing you learn on any course in critical methodology. {*Pause*} So, should I just ask people what they think about this? However, this wasn't part of the original project, and isn't really part of the interview guide, is it? Doesn't that make me a bad researcher?

CLINICAL PSYCHOLOGIST: Well, it is part of the interview guide to ask people what terms they feel comfortable with and what terms they want to use during the interview. In other words, you need to ask them what terms they use, or prefer to use, and how they feel about different umbrella terms such as 'intersex' and 'DSD', right?

RESEARCHER: That's true.

CLINICAL PSYCHOLOGIST: And no, you didn't really understand the importance of this question before coming to this point of your PhD process. But isn't that the whole idea of research – of really learning things and understanding that you might not know what the most important things are when you design the research?

RESEARCHER: Yes, that also feels like a take-home message from any course in qualitative methodologies. Okay. I'll talk to people and see what happens.

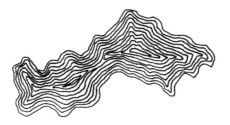

Still struggling as a PhD candidate in 2015

RESEARCHER TOVE: Okay, so I have done 22 interviews with young people and 33 interviews with parents.

CLINICAL PSYCHOLOGIST TOVE: Great! You were really struggling with terminology. What did people say?

RESEARCHER: Well, I am still struggling with terminology. I thought that I could talk to people about what terms they use and what they think about 'intersex' and 'DSD' so I would know what terms I should use in my thesis.

CLINICAL PSYCHOLOGIST: Well, how did it go?

RESEARCHER: Well, the conversations went well. It was quite easy to tune in to the specific thoughts and preferences of each participant. However, I'm still stuck, in a way. I still don't know what term, or terms, to use to write my thesis. And talking to these participants gave me a sense that none of the existing terms works for everyone and every occasion. So, I am still stuck.

CLINICAL PSYCHOLOGIST: Well, you have already submitted two articles. What did you write in them?

RESEARCHER: I tried to avoid the issue.

CLINICAL PSYCHOLOGIST: {*Sounding tired*} But, Tove, come on, you are trained as a clinical psychologist! You know that avoidance typically only helps you from a short-term perspective and that it often ends up not serving you in the longer run.

RESEARCHER: {*Frustrated*} I know! But what am I supposed to do? I don't have time to just sit and wait for some kind of eureka moment! I have 55 interviews to analyze! I need to publish my papers in order to finish my thesis! I only have like 18 months to go before I need to finish!

CLINICAL PSYCHOLOGIST: Okay. So I understand that you are under pressure and that you are very frustrated. And from what you are telling me, you have too much data and too little time. And I understand that this puts you in a position where you need to make choices as to what to focus on and not to focus on.

RESEARCHER: {Upset} EXACTLY!

CLINICAL PSYCHOLOGIST: But, I guess, you must have used some kind of terminology in those two submitted manuscripts. So could you tell me what you did?

RESEARCHER: {*Sighs*} Okay. In one paper (Lundberg *et al*. 2017), I focused only on a specific medical diagnosis, congenital adrenal hyperplasia (CAH). I said in the paper just that this diagnosis is usually covered under the umbrella term 'disorders of sex development' in medicine, but that terms such as 'intersex' and 'diverse sex development' are also used outside medicine. And then I just used the specific diagnostic term.

CLINICAL PSYCHOLOGIST: Well, it sounds like you were trying to be transparent and show the diversity here. So maybe not really 'avoiding the issue', but highlighting it and then not focusing on it in the paper? And in the other manuscript?

RESEARCHER: Well, in that paper (Lundberg *et al*. 2016) I stated that 'disorders of sex development' is used in medicine but that in psychology 'diverse sex development' is increasingly being used – which it was at the time. And then I used 'DSD', as meaning 'diverse sex development', in the article. I wrote this paper with two medical professionals and we had different opinions on what to use. They thought that using the formal medical language of 'disorders of sex development' was the best thing to do. But I just couldn't do that. My whole body just protested. It was just physically impossible! However, while I really appreciate the non-pathologizing sound of 'diverse sex development', I just think it doesn't do the job. It is perhaps the least-bad term, though.

CLINICAL PSYCHOLOGIST: Why do you think that 'diverse sex development' 'doesn't do the job'?

RESEARCHER: Well, this is complex. But, okay, this paper was a narrative analysis of the process of receiving a diagnosis. And 'diverse sex development' is not a diagnostic or medical term. Basically, all people with sex characteristics are covered by that term. So the title says 'a diagnosis related to diverse sex development', which is kind of a compromise. But I don't think that 'diverse sex development' will be able to replace 'disorders of sex development' because it is not referring to what medics want to refer to.

CLINICAL PSYCHOLOGIST: Okay, so what do medics want to refer to?

RESEARCHER: Well, in a medical consensus statement where 'disorders of sex development' is introduced as an umbrella term, it is to cover 'congenital conditions in which development of chromosomal, gonadal, or anatomic sex is atypical' (Lee *et al*. 2006, p. e488).

CLINICAL PSYCHOLOGIST: Okay, so do you think that 'disorder' is used as a synonym for 'congenital conditions'?

RESEARCHER: Well, I guess so. That this term was to point to conditions that might involve what medics would call pathological processes that 'abnormally affect physiology' (Pasterski *et al*. 2010, p. 189). I just feel that I have a different understanding of how words such as 'disorder' and 'abnormality' function than the people writing these things seem to have. I think these terms are really problematic. And at the same time I kind of get it. The whole healthcare system is built upon medical classifications. At least in Sweden, as soon as a doctor sees a patient, they need to report a diagnosis in the administrative system to be able to provide the patient with treatment and prescriptions, and also to get the correct funding to the relevant health centre or department.

CLINICAL PSYCHOLOGIST: Yes, this is how it works for us clinical psychologists as well in the healthcare system in Sweden.

RESEARCHER: Exactly. And it is so strange because, you know, the diagnosis can both be based on mutations in a gene, like the cause of a certain medical 'condition', *or* just the reason why someone sought healthcare. Diagnostic terminology is, in other words, formed on very different kinds of bases and the diagnostic system is philosophically very inconsistent.

CLINICAL PSYCHOLOGIST: Sure, causes for a condition and reasons why people seek help are very different.

RESEARCHER: Yes. However, I can't change that system, even though I think that 'disorders of sex development' is a bad term. But then again, if a medical umbrella term is really, really needed, I just think that they – we? – could have done some more work on the term. Like consulted someone who is a public relations specialist or something.

CLINICAL PSYCHOLOGIST: Okay. So what would be a better medical term, do you think, if you do the work?

RESEARCHER: Well, I don't know. But if they want to group diagnoses or conditions together in a classification, why not say just that? 'Conditions classified as affecting sex development'. I don't know. Or 'diagnoses classified as affecting sex development', and then they could keep the acronym DSD –

CLINICAL PSYCHOLOGIST: Sorry for interrupting your thoughts here, Tove. But have you written these things down?

RESEARCHER: What do you mean? No. Why?

CLINICAL PSYCHOLOGIST: Well, I am just thinking as your clinical part here again. You said that you avoided these issues. And I said to you that avoidance doesn't help you in the long term. If avoidance of something doesn't work, what should we do then?

RESEARCHER: What do you mean? Like generally? {*Thinking*} Well, the opposite of avoidance is exposure.

CLINICAL PSYCHOLOGIST: Yes. So, instead of trying to avoid this issue, should you engage in it? Should part of your argument in your thesis be about terminology? I mean, you did talk to people about their thoughts on terminology.

RESEARCHER: Yes, I did. But what do you mean – that this part of the data should be a specific paper?

CLINICAL PSYCHOLOGIST: Yes, for example. Why not?

RESEARCHER: {*Upset*} But I don't even know what to say?!

CLINICAL PSYCHOLOGIST: Well, you have already articulated several important points above. All of that could go into the introduction to the article. And then perhaps you need to engage with the data you have. I mean, what did people say?

RESEARCHER: I can't remember. Everyone just had very different thoughts and opinions. I need to go back and look at the data more systematically. Perhaps I can write a paper on people's preferences when it comes to terminology?

A couple of months later in 2015

RESEARCHER TOVE: Okay, I have some data for you.

CLINICAL PSYCHOLOGIST TOVE: Exciting! Tell me, what did they say?

RESEARCHER: Well, most participants don't talk about their characteristics. Not at all. And also many don't use certain labels to describe themselves. This young person explains it well {showing the clinical psychologist an excerpt from the transcription, see Box 1.1}:

BOX 1.1 EXCERPT FROM TRANSCRIPTION OF INTERVIEW WITH A YOUNG PERSON, CODED AS 'TERMINOLOGY'

Interviewer: I just wanted to hear like what words do you use when you talk about your development, or your condition, or…

Participant: I don't really talk about it that much. *{Laughter}* […]

Interviewer: No, no, so you don't really talk about it with other people, or…?

Participant: Um, I – I – no, not really, I think it's not a defining characteristic of myself.

Interviewer: No, no.

Participant: And I – maybe I've got to hide it a bit, but I don't think that actually it changes who I am and I shouldn't have to use these said words that, you know.

Interviewer: Yeah.

Participant: I'm just – you know, I'm just a bit different from other people […]. Sorry, that's probably not a very good answer, but…

Interviewer: It is a really good answer because, I mean, I'm interested in how you feel about things.

Participant: Yeah.

Interviewer: So that's – that's a perfectly fine answer.

Participant: Okay, good, good.

RESEARCHER: So now this is even more complex! I mean, researchers and professionals are kind of discussing {*talks in a silly voice*}, 'Do we need medical terms or not, and what should those be, and how about "intersex", and so on?', and in their everyday life many people don't really talk about it.

CLINICAL PSYCHOLOGIST: Yes. That sounds important.

RESEARCHER: Important? How?

CLINICAL PSYCHOLOGIST: Well, think as a clinician again. If you met a person who didn't talk about things, you would explore if there *is* a need to talk about things and the reasons for not talking about it. And if there is a need, you would try to make the unspoken 'talkable', right? And 'talkable' in different ways in different contexts? I mean, people have to be in many situations where they need to talk about these things.

RESEARCHER: Well, of course, participants said they needed to talk to their doctor or with partners and so on, and they did address how they dealt or didn't deal with that, in the interviews.

CLINICAL PSYCHOLOGIST: I think this part of the data is useful. It opens up something else about terminology.

RESEARCHER: Okay. How do you mean, 'opened up something else'?

CLINICAL PSYCHOLOGIST: Well, this is an interpretation and it might not be correct. But you have said that you feel very stuck when it comes to terminology, and that it is either 'DSD' OR 'intersex' and that you feel that choosing one or the other is problematic, but you can kind of see some of the points of both?

RESEARCHER: Yes, well, this is true.

CLINICAL PSYCHOLOGIST: So, first, you know, drawing on classic psychoanalytic thinking by Klein here (for an introduction to Klein, see e.g. Hinshelwood and Fortuna 2018), being stuck in an either/or position is typically problematic for people in the longer run. We need to be able to understand and integrate both aspects of, for example, the good and the bad in ourselves and others in order to function well. So I think that moving on from this either/or perspective to a more flexible one would be useful here. Second, I wonder if this 'stuckness' in terminology is just a parallel process, mirroring something about the phenomenon itself (see e.g. Sachs and Shapiro 1976).

RESEARCHER: Okay, so I think I got your first point. But this parallel process thing is a bit unclear.

CLINICAL PSYCHOLOGIST: Well, isn't the whole problem that binary understandings imply that sex characteristics need to be either male OR female, and so every kind of sense-making is based on that either/or construction?

RESEARCHER: Yes, and that is why it is called '*inter*sex'.

CLINICAL PSYCHOLOGIST: Yes. And so a psychodynamic interpretation of the terminology discussion is that this debate is stuck in the same dynamics, and perhaps also underpinned by the same socio-psychological forces as the understandings of sex characteristics themselves. The processes relevant for how we make sense of characteristics are also being played out in how we describe these characteristics. This is what we call 'parallel processes' in psychodynamic literature.

RESEARCHER: Okay, now it makes more sense. I haven't thought of it that way. But I think that this perspective could open something up. So the 'stuckness' I feel could be interpreted as not being about me only? I might be embodying larger and more fundamental things here?

CLINICAL PSYCHOLOGIST: Well, from a psychodynamic point of view, that could be an interpretation.

RESEARCHER: So maybe I don't need to 'choose' sides but explore if there are other ways of engaging with terminology.

CLINICAL PSYCHOLOGIST: Exactly. See if there are ways to open up conversations about terminology instead of being stuck.

RESEARCHER: This is potentially useful. {*Thinks for a while*} So when it comes to 'intersex' and 'DSD', one way of opening up the either/or dynamic would be to use both, like in 'intersex/DSD'? Instead of trying to find yet another term, like I was trying to do with 'atypical sex development'.

CLINICAL PSYCHOLOGIST: I guess different stakeholders will interpret that strategy in different ways, but yes, that is something else than choosing one term over the other or trying to sit in your room and 'invent yet another term'. Didn't you have a quote by a parent highlighting this?

RESEARCHER: Well, when I asked a parent what he thought about 'DSD' and said that health professionals and researchers use that as a standard term now, he replied {*reads quote*}: 'Fine – in your lab, do what you like. But when you're dealing with people, {*pause*} because you're so scientifically based, there's a whole group of people who can miss the fact that what you say […] can be incredibly hurtful.'

CLINICAL PSYCHOLOGIST: Ah, that's right. So if we think of ourselves as the ones in the 'lab', I really don't think that folks need yet another researcher suggesting a new term to use.

RESEARCHER: Yes, you have a point. Several young people also talked about the effects that terminology, especially 'disorders of sex development', could have on people. One young person said {*reading from transcript*}: 'I don't like the word "disorder", 'cause it suggests there's something wrong with someone. And for like, you know, some of these kids, […] if they hear "disorder of sexual development", they might, be it subconsciously or otherwise, think, "Oh my God", you know, […] "I've got something wrong with me".'

CLINICAL PSYCHOLOGIST: So that participant shared your concerns regarding 'disorder'.

RESEARCHER: Yes, but, at the same time, some also liked or used both 'DSD' and 'intersex'. Or they were very pragmatic. One parent said {*reads again*}: 'It's all jargon and […] recently they stopped saying "intersex" and started saying "DSD" […]. I'm comfortable with sort of all – all of the different terms […] it's whatever you want, so you know it's, if you want to identify as a person with a [DSD], then that's what you are; if you want to identify as intersex, that's what you are. […] ultimately, [our son] can decide […] how he talks about it. I think that's why I do want to almost talk about it in so many different ways.'

CLINICAL PSYCHOLOGIST: Tove, these are all really strong and important quotes. You need to write this terminology paper.

RESEARCHER: You think so? And illustrate the diversity and complexity of terminology instead of just descriptively summarize what terms people prefer?

CLINICAL PSYCHOLOGIST: Yes, definitely. You can also talk about what people prefer, but yes, highlight what people think. And also, I guess, the discrepancy between the formal terminology debate among professionals and the everyday sense-making and the communication needs that people have, which typically require another way of thinking about terminology. Like having a pool of different terms or ways of talking about your body in different contexts and for different purposes.

RESEARCHER: Yes. Another young person actually made that point really clear by saying that, whatever label is used by professionals, she is the one who needs to 'deal with it'. So yes, I guess I won't be able to avoid writing this paper.

Reflecting over reflexivity in retrospect: From 2019 and onwards

CLINICAL PSYCHOLOGIST TOVE: So, Tove, you wrote that paper eventually.

RESEARCHER TOVE: I did (Lundberg *et al.* 2018). And I positioned it as the first paper in my thesis. Like the foundation for the rest of the thesis.

CLINICAL PSYCHOLOGIST: And for the first time you have tried to put the process that led up to that paper into words in order to write about and evaluate your reflexivity in retrospect, as you said at the beginning of this chapter.

RESEARCHER: Yes.

CLINICAL PSYCHOLOGIST: So, the reconstructed section above really tries to make how you practised reflexivity and what theories you drew on transparent to the reader as well as yourself?

RESEARCHER: Yes, I hope it has made things more explicit. It is more apparent to me, at least. And, oh my, was that hard to write!

CLINICAL PSYCHOLOGIST: Why?

RESEARCHER: Well, first, it is hard to reconstruct something that happened a while ago. I think Hustvedt's quote at the beginning of the chapter illustrates that eloquently. And second, it was all so emotional and I really didn't know what to do with those feelings.

CLINICAL PSYCHOLOGIST: Yes, as a clinical psychologist, I can really see that you were struggling a lot with your feelings during your doctoral research. And I can see that it must have been emotional to return to those feelings as well. I wonder if you want to explore that a bit?

RESEARCHER: It was emotional! And being educated in a very post-positivist and quantitative discipline as a researcher, I interpret having all of these feelings as being biased and as being a bad researcher.

CLINICAL PSYCHOLOGIST: Okay, I see. So struggling with not only the emotions, but with not living up to a certain idea of how a researcher should be?

RESEARCHER: Yes! Exactly! And as an interdisciplinary scholar, maybe trying to navigate inconsistent and competing ideas of how a researcher should be? On the one hand, trying to adhere to those more quantitative ideals of my discipline and, on the other hand, trying to live up to ideals of being a critical and feminist scholar with social justice and ethics of care in mind.

CLINICAL PSYCHOLOGIST: I see. Yes, you mentioned feelings of 'in-between-ness' at the beginning of this chapter. It sounds like you were caught with challenging affects in between different epistemological ideals?

RESEARCHER: Yes, that is really how I felt.

CLINICAL PSYCHOLOGIST: Yes. And in the section above, where you reconstruct your experience of your doctoral work, there is also this sense of 'stuckness'. Now, when we talk, I still get an embodied feeling of being stuck.

RESEARCHER: Yes, in my academic work I tend to feel that I am walking on thin ice that might break at any minute. That I don't want to move, but have to, and do that slowly and just hope that the ice won't break.

CLINICAL PSYCHOLOGIST: That sounds daunting and… exhausting?

RESEARCHER: It is.

CLINICAL PSYCHOLOGIST: So, what does the walking-on-thin-ice metaphor symbolize right now?

RESEARCHER: Well, after writing the above section on my discomfort with terminology, it is really clear to me how my emotions kept me back, and how I tried to avoid them. And I am just not really sure what to do with all of these emotions in research? I mean, the main training I have had about emotions in research is that they shouldn't be there!

CLINICAL PSYCHOLOGIST: Sure, but you also mentioned critical and feminist theory. And several scholars in these traditions have, in fact, turned to affect.

RESEARCHER: Well, that is true.

CLINICAL PSYCHOLOGIST: And I know you know some of this literature, and that these scholars present very different ideas on emotions in research. For example, that emotions are not just an inevitable part of research, but perhaps even necessary. As in life in general. You know, as a clinical psychologist, I work a lot with affects because they 'move us to act or spur specific action' (McCullough et al. 2003, p. 15). In other words, we need affects to do things, for example to do research.

RESEARCHER: Yes, you are right. Hemmings (2012) refers to different theorists stressing the importance of rage, passion and other emotions, and highlights 'that in order to know differently, we have to feel differently' (p. 150). Similarly, Whitson (2017) points out that our emotional reactions to research say something about our 'dreams and desires' about ourselves and our 'research participants' (p. 305).

CLINICAL PSYCHOLOGIST: Exactly. However, I still feel that you are not really convinced that the emotions you experienced should have been there or even helped you during your PhD research?

RESEARCHER: No, I don't feel that they were really helping me! They were awful, and I wish I hadn't had to feel them!

CLINICAL PSYCHOLOGIST: Okay. I hear you. They weren't pleasant. I understand that not having to experience them at all would have been preferable. However, you also wondered if your practices of reflexivity actually made your research any better. Judging from our reconstruction of the discomfort with terminology, I would say that, yes, addressing this discomfort made the research better.

RESEARCHER: Why?

CLINICAL PSYCHOLOGIST: Because by exposing yourself and addressing this discomfort, instead of running away from it, you were able to know differently, just like Hemmings (2012) suggests.

RESEARCHER: Sure. I admit that addressing this discomfort provided me with a new route for my thesis. However, was it worth all the anguish and all the discomfort? Will I ever get rid of all of these negative feelings in the future? I don't know if I can stand being a researcher in the future if it means I will need to struggle like this in everything I do!

CLINICAL PSYCHOLOGIST: Well, maybe the problem is not that you have all of these feelings, but rather that you spend a lot of time and energy trying to avoid them?

RESEARCHER: Well, what is the alternative?

CLINICAL PSYCHOLOGIST: That you work with them.

RESEARCHER: How?

CLINICAL PSYCHOLOGIST: By acknowledging the fact that negative feelings and suffering are an inevitable part of life, including a part of doing research. And as human beings we tend to do two things in response to these feelings. One is to 'overidentify' with our feelings and perspectives: that how we feel and think *is how the world is* instead of *one* way of experiencing life. The other is to try to control or avoid feelings that make us suffer. However, these approaches can create more suffering because they make us psychologically inflexible. For instance, trying to control or get rid of unwanted aspects typically just creates more unwanted thoughts and feelings. Instead of reflecting, we might obsessively ruminate, for example.

RESEARCHER: That is exactly what I was trying to do. So what could an alternative way of relating to our emotions and thoughts be?

CLINICAL PSYCHOLOGIST: Well, if we draw on the understandings from some third-wave behavioural theories, first, we really need to connect to 'the ongoing flow of experience in the moment' (Hayes and Pierson 2005, p. 3). Instead of control or avoidance, we need to willingly accept that we will experience undesirable and negative situations and feelings. This also means exposing ourselves to discomfort instead of running away from it.

RESEARCHER: Okay. {*Thinking*} So, really we can't escape moments of discomfort in research? And drawing on this idea, this whole book could be understood as a collective exposure of discomfort where all the authors try to highlight it, instead of avoiding it? {*Laughing*}

CLINICAL PSYCHOLOGIST: {*Laughing*} Yes, that could be a constructive way of understanding this book.

RESEARCHER: Great! So what do we do next?

CLINICAL PSYCHOLOGIST: We practise developing a 'decentred stance' to cognitively defuse from our experiences, thoughts and feelings. By being non-judgmental and by not overidentifying with our feelings and thoughts, or trying to control or avoid them, we can develop a more flexible way of reflecting upon them and decide how to respond to our experiences. Instead of reacting automatically, this space gives us opportunities to do things that move us in a direction that is consistent with our values. However, this is a striving, a leaning towards something in life; these values are not specific goals that can be accomplished.

RESEARCHER: Well, it all sounds very clever, but it also sounds easier in theory than in practice?

CLINICAL PSYCHOLOGIST: It is a striving that you need to practise. It won't solve your discomfort, but it could help you deal with it in ways that are more constructive than trying to control or avoid things.

RESEARCHER: {*Quiet for a while*} So, let's see if I get what you are trying to say. Drawing on these theories, we, as researchers, need to understand that reflexivity is probably not something that would control or remove the moments of discomfort we experience. It isn't about becoming the perfect researcher with no flaws that will get things 'right' all the time? It is rather about accepting that we will mess up, experience defeat as well as success and sometimes be lucky enough to generate constructive knowledge? And that reflexivity could involve developing a 'decentred stance', from where we notice our experiences of research, and critically evaluate what we have written, our thinking, our practices and our feelings and see if what we do is in accordance with the values that we deeply care about as researchers? Also, in order to be accountable for what we do and our representations?

CLINICAL PSYCHOLOGIST: Yes, I think that is a reasonable summary of what I was trying to say.

RESEARCHER: I realize now that my preoccupation with trying to control or avoid my discomfort as well as my feelings of doing things wrong as a researcher actually was a source that led to a centring of myself. This is quite the opposite of what some writers, such as Skeggs (2002), suggest we do as reflexive researchers. If I had had more psychological flexibility via this 'decentred stance', I think I could have focused a lot more of my energy on knowledge production and my participants' concerns and accounts. To use the quote by Hemmings (2012, p. 150) again, 'in order to know differently' I would have had to feel differently about my feelings.

CLINICAL PSYCHOLOGIST: Well, being a researcher is challenging in several different ways. I think that not overidentifying with your discomfort and not interpreting these negative feelings as proof of your being a bad researcher would perhaps have made this work just a bit easier?

RESEARCHER: {Thinking} Perhaps. {Sits quietly for a while}

CLINICAL PSYCHOLOGIST: You are very quiet now.

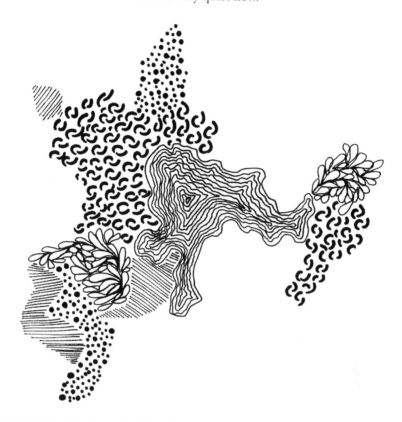

RESEARCHER: Yes. I am thinking about overidentifying with feelings. And how I felt about the terminology question.

CLINICAL PSYCHOLOGIST: What are you thinking?

RESEARCHER: Well, I think that, as a PhD candidate, I was still emotionally invested in finding 'The Term' that could be used by everyone, everywhere.

CLINICAL PSYCHOLOGIST: Yes, you really desired to 'solve' the terminology debate, didn't you?

RESEARCHER: I think I did, and I was quite disappointed in not being able to do it.

CLINICAL PSYCHOLOGIST: Well, that is a very natural response when people find things hard to contain. That you want something to be solved to escape the unbearable feelings it activates. When staying in the complexity is too over-whelming or when you are doing a lot of unrewarding 'dirty work', as Irvine (2014) calls it.

RESEARCHER: Yeah, that is probably it. I really do find this terminology discussion exhausting in many ways, and I think many others do as well. As soon as I talk to other researchers or health professionals about this, most don't really want to listen to or engage with the terminology discussion. It feels like many just want to decide on a term and then we can move on to discuss other 'more important' things.

CLINICAL PSYCHOLOGIST: Yes, well, as we discussed in the reconstructed part above, maybe it isn't about terminology *per se*, but about the phenomenon itself.

RESEARCHER: I think that interpretation makes sense. I think that I as a PhD candidate, in an embodied sense, experienced being 'amiss in how [some]one is recognized, feeling an ill fit with social descriptions', as Hemmings (2012, p. 150) calls it. However, it is only really in the last year that I have comprehended the width and depth of what this really means, also affectively.

CLINICAL PSYCHOLOGIST: Well, building on that, terminology sounds even more important to acknowledge in a thesis, then.

RESEARCHER: Yes, I think so. Liao (2015), who is a clinical psychologist and researcher, also talks about the need to start addressing emotions more explicitly in this topic area. She refers to healthcare, but I think we need to focus more on feelings in intersex research as well. If I were to write my thesis now, I would focus a bit more on different affective aspects and also try to utilize an affective reflexivity more explicitly.

CLINICAL PSYCHOLOGIST: Well, then, I understand why you think using your knowing as a clinical psychologist more explicitly would have been useful. Maybe you can do that in the future?

RESEARCHER: Maybe.

CLINICAL PSYCHOLOGIST: So, should that be the concluding remark of this chapter?

RESEARCHER: Ermmm… {*Hesitating*} If I am now supposed to follow your psychotherapeutic technique to connect to 'the ongoing flow of experience', which basically is the focus of this text now, I cannot avoid noticing some hesitations.

CLINICAL PSYCHOLOGIST: Great, let's notice them together.

RESEARCHER: Okay. So, in a way, I feel that the thoughts in this chapter are important. But I also just wonder how 'new' these ideas are, like methodologically? I mean, isn't this just some kind of introspective form of reflexivity, which has been criticized by so many academics (see e.g. Skeggs 2002, Pillow 2003)? Am I not just writing about my 'self' a lot now, which makes me self-centred and narcissistic as well as decentre what is important in my research?

CLINICAL PSYCHOLOGIST: What if it is narcissistic and self-centred?

RESEARCHER: Do you think it IS narcissistic?!

CLINICAL PSYCHOLOGIST: Well, I think that it is possible to interpret it in different ways. And I guess some would say that academia is quite narcissistic. And speaking of that, let's think about your hesitation to write about your 'self'. You are working in a system where the best success indicator of who you are as an academic is the texts you are writing. So, in this system, the impression-management of your 'self' is what you have got to deal with. Is that narcissistic? Then, yes.

RESEARCHER: But being in academia doesn't mean that I have to centre myself in everything I do, does it? And I just wonder if there is too much centring of myself in this text?!

CLINICAL PSYCHOLOGIST: Well, you did make it clear that you wanted to use this chapter to explore your reflexivity during your PhD research. So, one interpretation could be that this is a self-centred and confessional piece. But maybe you and others can still learn from it?

RESEARCHER: Well, I certainly have learned something in writing this chapter. But maybe I should have done this work quietly and privately in my office?

CLINICAL PSYCHOLOGIST: Well, that is what you said you did as a PhD candidate, didn't you? And then you were worried about not being reflexive enough.

RESEARCHER: Fair point.

CLINICAL PSYCHOLOGIST: Or maybe it isn't narcissistic? Another interpretation could be that maybe it is not only your 'self' that is in focus here, but rather your thinking and your knowing? But these are, of course, related to your 'self'. By that I mean, as I think Skeggs (2002) points out, the self is a historically and socially produced 'necessity' nowadays, isn't it? I mean, can you 'escape' your 'self', even though we can clearly see that this is part of a certain discourse? Can you step outside of discourse? As far as how I understand Foucault (1984), you can't. And do you really focus on your 'self' or is it not your 'subjectivity'? And what is really the difference?

RESEARCHER: Okay, I see the complexity here. These are all really hard and important questions. And they are not really new questions, either...

CLINICAL PSYCHOLOGIST: Well, your hesitation about this chapter being 'new': I don't think this is new. Does everything you write have to be 'new'? And what does 'new' even mean? Does it mean ideas, words or meanings that have never been expressed before? Always writing something new seems like a very hopeless and tiring ideal for an academic.

RESEARCHER: It is a very hopeless and tiring thing to be an academic!

CLINICAL PSYCHOLOGIST: Then should you perhaps stop overidentifying with these ideals and start to 'decentre' from them a bit?

RESEARCHER: Actually, I'm not sure I will be able to do that. But sure, I'll try.

CLINICAL PSYCHOLOGIST: Well, trying is all we can do. Remember that being in a 'decentred stance' as well as living and researching in your valued direction is a striving, a leaning towards something in life. It isn't a goal that can be reached once and for all time.

RESEARCHER: Okay, sure. So, I will try to decentre from problematic academic ideals but still reflect on and engage with them. And I hope that the readers of this book will too.

CLINICAL PSYCHOLOGIST: Well, social support is one of the most effective coping strategies there are. You all know that from writing this book.

RESEARCHER: That is true.

CLINICAL PSYCHOLOGIST: So, can the clinical psychologist share a final professional tip, then?

RESEARCHER: Sure, go on!

CLINICAL PSYCHOLOGIST: I suggest that you all continue resisting these problematic academic ideals together.

RESEARCHER: Collective resistance via affective reflexivity? {*Pause*} I like that. I'm on!

Notes

1 'Moments of discomfort', which is part of the title of this book, sounds like a good descriptive summary of the feelings of disorientation, frustration and 'stuckness' I experienced as a doctoral researcher in psychology from 2012 to 2017. The discomfort was mostly related to my attempts to position myself in a field of research where at least two very different bodies of knowledge with contrasting views are evident. The topic of my thesis was to explore the lived experiences of people with sex characteristics that do not conform to typical understandings of female or male physical development (Lundberg 2017). Within medicine, such characteristics are typically referred to as 'disorders of sex development' that are understood to be 'congenital conditions in which development of chromosomal, gonadal, or anatomic sex is atypical' (Lee *et al.* 2006, p. e488). The term 'intersex', however, is used by many people with personal experience of DSD as well as by human rights advocates and researchers within the humanities and the social sciences (Lundberg *et al.* 2018). In these contexts, intersex characteristics are understood as naturally occurring variations of human embodiment that should be recognized and protected by human rights. One main challenge that gave rise to the discomfort was to stay in conversation with both of these perspectives and at the same time try to articulate my own position in an intelligible manner. The different participants whom I interviewed for this project, 22 young people and 33 parents, described very different challenges in their everyday lives, presented diverse ways of making sense of their or their child's variations and preferred different terminology to describe these characteristics (Lundberg *et al.* 2018). Some participants drew on medical discourses and labelled themselves or their child as someone with a specific medical condition. Others articulated thoughts that were more in line with the human rights perspective and some young people also identified as intersex. Only some participants utilized both discourses. A challenge during my research was thus to respect the many different ways that participants made sense of their embodiment, while at the same time critically analyze and discuss the medical *as well as* the human rights perspective. Being caught in a dilemma of respecting research participants while at the same time, on a more general level, problematizing and criticizing the same frameworks of understanding that participants draw on is not a unique or new challenge. Feminist scholars have struggled with these issues for decades (Wilkinson and Kitzinger 1996, Finlay 2002a). However, even though I think I was able to articulate some kind of strategy in dealing with these moments of discomfort, I still feel that my 'solution' was very provisional. Finally, I was also discomforted when I was trying to put all of the above-mentioned discomfort, and the ways I coped with it, into words. As a young clinical psychology student, I was encouraged to do such reflexive work when I saw clients; however, I was never trained to do so when I did research. The formal and expected requirements of the thesis and the lack of time and skills of understanding how I was to 'write about reflexivity' led me to omit the reflexive parts I initially planned to have in the introduction to my thesis. In other words, I retreated from engaging with reflexivity (Finlay 2002b). This chapter starts in the discomfort related to reflexivity and the chapter's main aim is to write about those reflexive parts that were omitted in my thesis.

2 While it looks like all these conversations happened in my head, they did not appear in an academic vacuum. Many of the insights presented in this chapter have been possible because of other people's input. I could never have arrived at these thoughts if it were not for Katrina Roen, Peter Hegarty, Lih-Mei Liao, Margaret Simmonds, Ellie Magritte, Del LaGrace Volcano and many others. I am also deeply thankful for conversations with Catrine Andersson and Elinor Hermansson, which have helped me feel differently about my feelings.

3 Narrating a history of intersex in order to provide a background and a context for the current situation is a complex task. Narrations in current academic texts usually use the paradigm of medical guidelines from the 1950s (the ones suggested by Money, Hampson and Hampson 1955) and describe the growing critique of researchers (such as Fausto-Sterling 1993, Diamond and Sigmundson 1997, Kessler 1998) and activists (such as Chase 1998) during the 1990s as the starting point for the current situation. Narrations also often point out that these developments led many stakeholders to be concerned about medical practices by the beginning of the 2000s (Davis 2015). One main discussion since then has been in regard to whether early surgery should be performed in order to normalize the appearance of children's genitals. Other aspects that are typically narrated as important parts of the changes that have happened since the 1990s include discussions on how to understand these variations, what terminology to use, and if, and in that case how, medical classifications should be constructed. Many authors, for example Dreger (1999), Karkazis (2008), Reis (2012), Davis (2015) and Garland (2016), provide important historical contextualizations. When it comes to terminology, activists reclaimed the term 'intersex' as well as 'hermaphrodite' from medicine in the 1990s (Davis 2015). In 2005, activists, bioethicists and medical practitioners wrote a piece together arguing for a revision in terminology and medical classifications (Dreger *et al.* 2005). Their main point was that the diagnostic taxonomy, including terms such as 'hermaphroditism' and 'pseudo-hermaphroditism', was problematic because the terms were based on the histology of gonads and, thus, scientifically misleading as well as stigmatizing. They suggested a system where specific conditions were recognized and that these could be grouped together with the medical umbrella term 'disorders of sexual differentiation' (DSD). This suggestion was taken up by medical experts. Also in 2005, a consensus meeting with paediatricians and a couple of patient representatives was held in Chicago. A year later, a Consensus statement was published (Lee *et al.* 2006). In this document, the umbrella term 'disorders of sex development' (DSD) was presented as well as a new taxonomy that classified specific conditions on the basis of chromosomes. The authors argued that 'disorders of sex development' was a better term than 'intersex' because it was more descriptive and because it incorporated advances in medicine. It was also understood as less confusing and stigmatizing as well as more meaningful to the people concerned. Since the early 2000s, different groups that organize people with lived experiences of intersex/DSD have appeared and some have changed their format and approach (Davis 2015). Some are organized as support groups and work in close collaboration with health providers and medical researchers in order to improve care. Some of these groups support the current medical terminology and taxonomy as well as the guidelines and practices. While not all groups understand DSD as 'disorders of sex development', but rather as 'diverse' or 'differences of sex development' (Monro *et al.* 2017), some still support the idea that these variations can or should be understood from a medical model. Other organizations have continued to criticize medical practices. Some of these latter groups ground their claims in human rights (Ghattas 2015). With the support of international LGBTQ organizations, some groups argue that the still-occurring practices of non-essential surgery violate children's rights to bodily integrity and self-determination (a concern also raised by the United Nations Human Rights Council 2013). Commentators are also critical of the changes in medical terminology and classifications (see e.g. Davis 2014, Monro *et al.* 2017). They argue that this medical reclassification pathologizes variations in embodiment which, in turn, underpins problematic medical practices. Some also argue that the continuous medicalization of these sex characteristics gives medical professionals a disproportionate amount of power in defining how these variations should be understood and also treated. As such, the move towards using the term 'DSD' in medicine can be understood as a form of hermeneutical

injustice, where the right to self-determination in understanding and naming one's body and oneself has been taken away from people with these sex characteristics (Carpenter 2016). It was in the context of these complexities that my doctoral thesis was situated.

References

Alvesson, M. and Sköldberg, K., 2017. *Tolkning och reflektion: Vetenskapsfilosofi och kvalitativ metod [Interpretation and reflection: Philosophy of science and qualitative method]*. Lund: Studentlitteratur.

Carpenter, M., 2016. The human rights of intersex people: Addressing harmful practices and rhetoric of change. *Reproductive Health Matters*, 24 (47), 74–84. doi: 10.1016/j. rhm.2016.06.003.

Chase, C., 1998. Hermaphrodites with attitude: Mapping the emergence of Intersex political activism. *GLQ: A Journal of Lesbian and Gay Studies*, 4 (2), 189–211.

Davis, G., 2014. The power in a name: Diagnostic terminology and diverse experiences. *Psychology & Sexuality*, 5 (1), 15–27. doi: 10.1080/19419899.2013.831212.

Davis, G., 2015. *Contesting intersex: The dubious diagnosis*. New York, NY: New York University Press.

Diamond, M. and Sigmundson, H.K., 1997. Sex reassignment at birth. *Archives of Pediatrics and Adolescent Medicine*, 151 (3), 298–304. doi:10.1001/archpedi.1997.02170400084015.

Doucet, A. and Mauthner, N.S., 2007. Feminist methodologies and epistemology. In C. D. Bryant & D. L. Peck (Eds.), *Handbook of 21st Century sociology*, Vol. 2. Thousand Oaks, CA: SAGE, 36–45.

Dreger, A.D., 1999. *Intersex in the age of ethics*. Hagerstown, MD: University Pub. Group.

Dreger, A.D. et al., 2005. Changing the nomenclature/taxonomy for intersex: A scientific and clinical rationale. *Journal of Pediatric Endocrinology and Metabolism*, 18 (8), 729. doi:10.1515/JPEM.2005.18.8.729.

Fausto-Sterling, A., 1993. The five sexes: Why male and female are not enough. *The Sciences*, 33 (2), 20–24. doi:10.1002/j.2326-1951.1993.tb03081.x.

Finlay, L., 2002a. Negotiating the swamp: The opportunity and challenge of reflexivity in research practice. *Qualitative Research*, 2 (2), 209–230. doi:10.1177/146879410200200205.

Finlay, L., 2002b. 'Outing' the *Researcher*: The provenance, process and practice of reflexivity. *Qualitative Health Research*, 12 (4), 531–545. doi:10.1177/104973202129120052.

Foucault, M., 1984. *The history of sexuality 1: An introduction*. Harmondsworth: Penguin.

Garland, J., 2016. *On science, law, and medicine: The case of gender-'normalizing' interventions on children who are diagnosed as different in sex development*. Thesis (PhD). Uppsala University.

Ghattas, D.C., 2015. *Standing up for the human rights of intersex people – How can you help?* Available from: http://www.ilga-europe.org/sites/default/files/how_to_be_a_great_intersex_ally_a_toolkit_for_ngos_and_decision_makers_december_2015_updated.pdf [Accessed 27 October 2020].

Hayes, S.C. and Pierson, H., 2005. Acceptance and commitment therapy. In S. Felgoise, A. M. Nezu, C. M. Nezu, & M. A. Reinecke (Eds.), *Encyclopedia of cognitive behavior therapy*. London: Springer, 1–4.

Hemmings, C., 2012. Affective solidarity: Feminist reflexivity and political transformation. *Feminist Theory*, 13 (2), 147–161. doi:10.1177/1464700112442643.

Hinshelwood, R.D. and Fortuna, T., 2018. *Melanie Klein: The basics*. New York, NY: Routledge.

Hollway, W. and Jefferson, T., 2011. *Doing qualitative research differently: Free association, narrative and the interview method*. Los Angeles, LA: SAGE.

Hustvedt, S., 2019. *Memories of the future*. New York, NY: Simon & Schuster.

Irvine, J.M., 2014. Is sexuality research 'dirty work'? Institutionalized stigma in the production of sexual knowledge. *Sexualities*, 17 (5–6), 632–656.

Karkazis, K., 2008. *Fixing sex: Intersex, medical authority, and lived experience*. Durham, NC: Duke University Press.

Kessler, S.J., 1998. *Lessons from the intersexed*. New Brunswick, NJ: Rutgers University Press.

Lee, P.A. et al., 2006. Consensus statement on management of intersex disorders. In collaboration with the participants in the International Consensus Conference on Intersex organized by the Lawson Wilkins Pediatric Endocrine Society and the European Society for Paediatric Endocrinology. *Pediatrics*, 118 (2), e488–e500. doi:10.1542/peds.2006-0738.

Liao, L.M., 2015. Stonewalling emotion. *Narrative Inquiry in Bioethics*, 5 (2), 143–150.

Lundberg, T., 2017. *Knowing bodies: Making sense of Intersex/DSD a decade post-consensus*. Thesis (PhD). University of Oslo. Available from: https://www.duo.uio.no/handle/10852/55654 [Accessed 27 October 2020].

Lundberg, T. et al., 2016. 'It's part of me, not all of me': Young women's experiences of receiving a diagnosis related to diverse sex development. *Journal of Pediatric and Adolescent Gynecology*, 29 (4), 338–343. doi:10.1016/j.jpag.2015.11.009.

Lundberg, T. et al., 2017. From knowing nothing to knowing what, how and now: Parents' experiences of caring for their children with congenital adrenal hyperplasia. *Journal of Pediatric Psychology*, 42 (5), 520–529. doi:10.1093/jpepsy/jsw001.

Lundberg, T., Hegarty, P. and Roen, K., 2018. Making sense of 'Intersex' and 'DSD': How laypeople understand and use terminology. *Psychology & Sexuality*, 9 (2), 161–173. doi:10.1080/19419899.2018.1453862.

McCullough, L. et al., 2003. *Treating affect phobia: A manual for short-term dynamic psychotherapy*. New York, NY: Guilford Press.

Money, J., Hampson, J.G. and Hampson, J.L., 1955. Hermaphroditism: Recommendations concerning assignment of sex, change of sex and psychologic management. *Bulletin of the Johns Hopkins Hospital*, 97 (4), 284–300.

Monro, S. et al., 2017. *Intersex, variations of sex characteristics, and DSD: The need for change*. Available from: http://eprints.hud.ac.uk/id/eprint/33535 [Accessed 27 October 2020].

Pasterski, V., Prentice, P. and Hughes, I.A., 2010. Impact of the consensus statement and the new DSD classification system. *Best Practice & Research: Clinical Endocrinology & Metabolism*, 24 (2), 187–195.

Pillow, W., 2003. Confession, catharsis, or cure? Rethinking the uses of reflexivity as methodological power in qualitative research. *International Journal of Qualitative Studies in Education*, 16 (2), 175–196.

Reis, E., 2012. *Bodies in doubt: An American history of intersex*. Baltimore, MD: Johns Hopkins University Press.

Sachs, D.M. and Shapiro, S.H., 1976. On parallel processes in therapy and teaching. *The Psychoanalytic Quarterly*, 45 (3), 394–415.

Schön, D.A., 1995. *The reflective practitioner: How professionals think in action*. Aldershot: Arena.

Skeggs, B., 2002. Techniques for telling the reflexive self. In: T. May, ed. *Qualitative research in action*. London: SAGE, 349–374.

United Nations Human Rights Council, 2013. *Report of the special rapporteur on torture and other cruel, inhuman or degrading treatment or punishment, Juan E. Méndez* (A/HRC/22/53). Available from: http://www.ohchr.org/Documents/HRBodies/HRCouncil/RegularSession/Session22/A.HRC.22.53_English.pdf [Accessed 27 October 2020].

Whitson, R., 2017. Painting pictures of ourselves: Researcher subjectivity in the practice of feminist reflexivity. *The Professional Geographer*, 69 (2), 299–306.

Wilkinson, S. and Kitzinger, C., 1996. *Representing the other: A Feminism & psychology reader*. London: SAGE.

2

'TO SAY NO WASN'T SOMETHING WE COULD DO'

Reflexive accounts and negotiations of the ethical practice of informed consent during the research process and beyond

Johanna Sixtensson

To: Johanna.sixtensson@mau.se
On: Friday, 6 April 2018 at 10.09
Subject: Hello!

I received your book today and I must say I was shocked. I thought I had received someone else's post. But while reading I started to remember and I couldn't stop reading. It was very interesting, and fun to read my own words. 6–7 years have passed since the interview with you and a lot has changed when it comes to us, of course. We are still friends and see each other when we can. Some of us still study […] and others (me) have travelled every other month and enjoyed life.

The reason why I write (besides to say that I was very impressed with your work) is that I want to explain why we were so difficult to get hold of or didn't appear at the interviews… We were interested; but just then we were young, lazy girls who simply couldn't bother. We were 16–17 years old, and a little disrespectful. Today, we would never have done what we did back then […]. And to say no wasn't something we could do. So, we ignored you and felt bad instead.

I think you deserve to know it and I was embarrassed when I read about it in the book. I'm sorry it made you frustrated. But I'm glad you managed to see the positives in it all. At least, I gave you the correct number the second time (haha) […].

Good luck with the rest of your life ☺

Kind Regards,
'Leila'

The above extract is from an e-mail from a research participant to whom I gave the name Leila. I first met her during the autumn of 2012. At that time, she was 17 years old and I was visiting her class at a secondary school to inform them about my research project and ask for participants. I was conducting research on teenage girls' lived experiences of everyday life in in the city of Malmö in southern Sweden. A few weeks after my first visit to the class, Leila and three of her friends participated in a focus group. A few months later, in January 2013, I met her again for an individual interview. After that, our paths parted and we had no further contact until March 2018, when I sent my published book to her and the other research participants. Along with the printed book I attached a handwritten note where I mentioned the long time that had passed since I last saw them and thanked them for their participation. On the note I included my e-mail address in case they had any questions.

At the beginning of April 2018, Leila's e-mail reached my inbox. Approximately 5 years had passed since I interviewed her and she must have been 22 or 23 when she wrote to me. Even though participant responses to research findings are always a possibility, and I had opened up the possibility for exactly this by sending out the book and my e-mail address along with it, Leila's reaching out to me took me by surprise. I remember feeling grateful and moved that she had taken time not only to read the book, but also to write to me and comment on aspects of its content. Mixed up with this positive response of mine was also a more uncomfortable feeling that originated in our past meetings, that was also one of my biggest methodological dilemmas during the research process. The essence of the problem is located in Leila's saying: 'to say no wasn't something we could do' and refers back to my seeking *informed consent* as it would be a verbal, linear and rational one-time decision, and then getting mixed, not always verbal, signals in return. This, at the time of the fieldwork, was frustrating, confusing and stressful. However, taking time to theoretically *think* about the meaning of the concept of consent, and analyzing the events that took place between me and the participants through that lens, has led to a broader understanding. To consent, or not, I argue, is rather an open-ended, situated, ambivalent and not necessarily verbal process that requires a situated ethical (re)thinking on the researcher's part.

The Swedish Centre for Research Ethics & Bioethics on its online site states that 'When research involves humans, they are, with few exceptions, to be informed about the research and its effects, as well as being able to freely decide whether they wish to participate' (CODEX 2020). This information, moreover, should be given in a neutral manner in order not to put pressure on possible participants. As a PhD student within social sciences using qualitative methods in planning and conducting my first individual research project, I anxiously tried to follow the formal criteria for this ethical principle. It turned out to be difficult since, even though the guidelines of the ethical principle of informed consent make it seem like a straightforward, linear and rational process (Gallagher *et al.* 2010), the practice of informed consent, asking for it and giving it, is a 'slippery and elusive notion during the research process' (Aaltonen 2017, p. 329), as will be elaborated in this chapter. Throughout the text, I will revisit, explore and make meaning of methodological and ethical dilemmas connected to the principle of informed consent that took place between Leila, her group of friends and me, but that to some extent were present in encounters with other participants too. At the core of the discussion will be the complex researcher–participant relationship during the research process and beyond, a relationship that is imbued with power dynamics, expectations and affects. The writing of this chapter I regard as not only an important reflexive practice but also an ambition to strive for a more ethical representation of my research participants, making their expressions of agency visible in a text that involves their narratives, or, as McGarry puts it: 'active in the construction and negotiation of their own biographies' (2016, p. 352).

Research topic and challenges of the recruitment procedure

The research project I will be describing constituted my doctoral dissertation (Sixtensson 2018) in which, from a qualitative and in-depth perspective using interviews and focus groups as methods, I examined the everyday life of a group of teenage girls between 16 and 19 years old. The analytical focus of the research was on how the young women encountered and negotiated with unequal socio-spatial gender structures, class relations and processes of racialization in their everyday lives. Some of the participating girls, among them Leila and her group of friends, had parents with migrant background and had experiences of being constructed as 'non-Swedish' or 'foreigners' due to bodily features such as skin colour. As will be seen throughout the text, I regard these racialized experiences as especially important concerning some of the incidents that took place between Leila, her group of friends and me.

The fieldwork conducted for the project was quite challenging: to some extent, it was difficult to locate participants, but the main problem was to schedule and conduct interviews and focus groups. I got in contact with potential research participants through secondary schools as well as through different youth activities in the municipality of Malmö. Via e-mail, I asked for permission to visit classes or groups to inform them about my research project and ask for participants. To gain access was not as easy as I had imagined beforehand. However, when I was given access to a classroom or some other place, I described the project and asked for voluntary participants for a focus group discussion and, possibly later on, an individual interview. As far as I perceived it, I generally succeeded in gaining the young women's interest to participate, and often they would expressly say so and/ or give me their contact details. Trying to organize focus groups and interviews, however, was very difficult. Participants cancelled at short or long notice or just did not show up at our planned meetings. On two occasions, no one came to scheduled focus groups. These complications, which at the time felt like rejections, affected my self-esteem and led me to question my ability to do this kind of research. They also caused stress in relation to the time aspects of the research project. Before I analytically explore these difficulties and my reactions to them, both back then and with hindsight, I will present the specific circumstances that characterized the relationship between me, Leila and her group of friends.

Fake phone numbers and on-and-off communication: a timeline

The first time I met Leila was when I visited her class at a secondary school. I had arranged with her class teacher to come and inform them about the project and ask for participants. I did so and, when I left, I had with me the names and phone numbers of eight individuals, who had written them down on a piece of paper that I had passed around at the end of the information session. We did not set a date for the focus group there and then, but I said that I would contact them. When I did, I got in touch with four or five out of the eight young women and arranged a time and place for a focus group. However, at the scheduled focus group none of the young women showed up. After some consideration, I decided to try to get in contact with this group of individuals again in the hope of rescheduling the focus group discussion. I had come to learn that it was difficult to arrange dates for discussions that suited everyone by phone or text messages, and therefore decided to send an e-mail to the class teacher who had welcomed me to the class, asking her if I could come back and try to organize a new time for the focus group with the young women present in the room and, preferably, set a time for it to be held at the end of a school day. She invited me to come again and do so. Still, I had doubts, partly due to my fear that the teacher would have an impact on the young women's decision to participate. My uncertainty was also, at this point, partly because I felt that by approaching them in their school again I might force myself on them. In the end, however, I decided to go ahead and visit the class once more. The basis of my decision to do so was that the young women who signed up the first time *had*, in my interpretation, seemed genuinely interested to participate in the focus group. Would I not let them down if I withdrew myself solely due to the fact that none of them had turned up the first time? Accordingly, I entered the classroom again. The teacher introduced me, but left the classroom when it was my time to talk to the young women, as I had asked her to do. In the fieldnotes made after my second visit, I wrote:

> I told them that I would still like to meet them for one focus group discussion, something that is totally voluntary. I suggested we do this in connection with the end of a school day. I also said that I wished to talk only to the ones who

were interested, and I underlined again that it is voluntary. I said that the ones who were still interested to talk to me could stay on and the others could leave. Four girls stayed […]. One of them said, 'I have a great deal to say' when I yet again briefly told them about the project and what we would discuss in the focus group.

From the notes, I can see that I was anxious, stressing the voluntary aspect of participating several times. At the time, this was my way of trying to secure the formalities of *informed consent* that I had learned, in research with young participants especially, should be addressed and readdressed several times throughout the process (Gallagher *et al.* 2010). The girl who said 'I have a great deal to say' was Leila; and as the focus group took place shortly after this meeting, to my relief she and her three friends showed up as agreed upon.

We met up outside their school and walked a short distance to a public building where I had booked a room for us to conduct the focus group discussion. Leila, as well as the rest of the group, did have a lot to say, as Leila had stated. Two central themes of discussion concerned the young women's experiences of living in a neighbourhood that is discursively constructed as 'deprived' and about experiences of encounters of *everyday racism*. In connection with the theme of *everyday racism*, it is vital to highlight that such experiences, with regard to the whole research project, were articulated almost exclusively in focus group discussions. When I readdressed the topic in individual interviews, their accounts were short. In the focus group, however, experiences of racism were often articulated in unanimity and in a sort of collective agreement. The young women would finish each other's sentences, used the pronouns 'we' or 'us' and sometimes nodded in agreement as they described these experiences. In the focus group that Leila participated in, an example of this consensus could be seen in the following quote:

> *LEILA:* I have also seen several times when we are out shopping that –
> *SEVERAL IN THE GROUP:* Yes.
> *LEILA:* the staff, they keep an eye on you all the time.
> *KAMILA:* They follow you around.
> *LEILA:* They think you'll nick stuff, and it's really humiliating, just because we are foreigners.

In this particular quote, it is consumer experiences that collectively are described as involving degrading treatment for this group of participants. A similar pattern of communicating collective experiences, using 'we', is evident in the group's discussions of experiences of living in neighbourhoods that are described in negative terms as violent, deprived and unsafe, a theme that they also discussed intensely. At the end of the focus group, Leila said to me: 'Do you know what would have been good? […] some advice from me to you: that we, four "foreigners", tell our side and if you interview a group of "Swedes" [too].' The other participants nodded to her proposal. I answered in an affirmative way, that to talk to young women with different backgrounds and experiences was what I planned to do. American ethnographer Julie Bettie (2014) writes about a similar experience in a study that, interestingly enough, also concerned teenage females with different backgrounds. One of Bettie's participants says something similar to Leila: 'you can't just write about the white girls. It would only be half a story, half a book' (Bettie 2014, p. 22). Leila, like the young woman in Bettie's study, seemed to be well aware of the differences that are likely to appear if her and her group of friends' experiences are put in comparison with white young women's narratives of everyday life, and she was actively asking me not to neglect these *differences*. As we ended the discussion, I asked the participants if they would be happy to meet me for individual interviews. I felt enthusiastic about, among other things, getting the chance to deepen some of the discussions into a more personal angle during individual interviews. In my notes made after the focus group discussion, I wrote:

> They had a lot to say, interrupting each other as well as completing each other's sentences [...]. All of them agreed to hold an individual interview with me. The proposal was to do this on Tuesdays when they have a free period in in their school schedule. I got their phone numbers again.

However, when I tried to organize these interviews, I managed to contact only one of them, which was Leila. As for the other three, I discovered when I compared their phone numbers, collected on two occasions, that they did not match and/or were incorrect. Even Leila, I learnt, had left me two different phone numbers, one incorrect and one that was actually hers. To get in touch with one of the young women whom I was particularly interested to interview, I sent a text message to Leila and asked if she could put me in contact with the young woman, since the number I had got from her was wrong. Within a few minutes, I received a number attached to a text message. I was astonished when I realized that that number as well was incorrect. In the end, I managed to obtain an interview with Leila, but I let the others go, not making any further attempts to reach them. In my fieldnotes, I wrote:

> What's the reason for their doing this? They seem to be very close to each other, they have known each other since kindergarten; have they developed a code for faking their phone numbers? Why don't they tell me they don't want to, if they don't want to see me? Are they making fun of me, or daren't they say no?

As seen from my notes, I tried to understand and make meaning of these incidents early on. The possibility of not being able, or not daring, to say no was already on my mind; and since for the whole project I was interested in young women's means of agency and resistance, I was at first frustrated, but later intrigued, by what looked like sophisticated actions set up to mislead me.

I met Leila again a few months later. She had agreed to an individual interview and we yet again met outside her school. She gave me a hug and we entered the school building and into a separate room which she had suggested for the interview. Once more, I repeated the voluntary aspects of participation before starting the interview. Leila answered all my questions, but was not as talkative as in the focus group, which surprised me somewhat, as she was the one who had talked the most then. However, now, her answers were not as developed and some of the themes, such as experiences of everyday racism that had been intensely discussed during the focus group, as I readdressed them, gave rise to only short accounts.[1] She seemed to get restless as time passed and said by way of explanation that she had just stopped smoking. I ended the interview after an hour, slightly earlier than I wanted to. As we walked out of the school building together, I thanked her and after that we parted ways.

I continued to conduct more interviews with other participants before moving on to analytical work and the long process of writing the doctoral thesis. As the text eventually started to develop, narratives from Leila and her group of friends were given quite a large amount of textual space, and in the methodological section of the thesis I addressed and tried briefly to make meaning of the incidents with the fake phone numbers. Leila's e-mail, which starts off this chapter, and my reply, could have been the end of our on-and-off communication; however, when embarking on this chapter, I was given the opportunity to reach out yet again to ask Leila if I could include parts of her e-mail in a text about dilemmas in conducting focus groups and interviews. Only a few minutes after I sent my e-mail, her reply reached my inbox stating: '*that's fine!* ☺ '.

Complexities and contradictions of consent in theory and practice

In the following section, I will try to make meaning of the incidents where Leila and her friends were difficult to get hold of, giving me incorrect phone numbers, and how they, even though they initially agreed to participate, later on *acted* as if they had not. At the centre of the discussion will be the question, 'why did they not just *say* no?' and how this relates to power relations at play as well as the ethical principle of informed consent, in theory and practice. Within the disciplinary field of children's geographies, there are valuable methodological discussions about the shifting (as opposed to fixed) power relations between researcher and young participants during the research process (cf. Skelton 2008). Holt (2004) argues that the research contains shifting, contextual and embodied 'research performances'. Woodyer, too, maintains that research encounters should be reframed as performances in order to understand and deconstruct the idea of a necessarily hierarchical relationship between researcher and research participant. Instead, she argues that research encounters are a constant negotiation: 'It is seen that power relations cannot be reduced to powerful and powerless along essentialized lines of difference. Rather, power is fluid; it is performed, and thus open to negotiation' (2008, p. 352).

Drawing on the knowledge production on the concept of consent concerning sexual situations from the field of sexuality studies, David Archard (1998) discusses the meaning of this concept in a broad sense. He makes an interesting distinction between the concept of *consent* and the similar concept of *assent*, arguing that, while consent is 'agreement *to* something', assent is more than that: assent is 'agreement *with* something'. Unlike consent, assent is an act as well as a 'state of mind'. In a similar way, Hickman and Muehlenhard, also coming from the field of sexualities, describe consent as both a mental and physical practice: to make a decision and convey this decision (Hickman and Muehlenhard 1999). Moreover, consent, within this field, is described as a dynamical, complex and continuous process. To consent, then, is not a fixed decision but an open-ended process (Gunnarsson 2020). In 'Just say no? The use of Conversation Analysis in developing a feminist Perspective on sexual refusal' (1999), Kitzinger and Frith draw on literature that has applied Conversation Analysis (CA) to study individuals' means of 'saying no' in everyday interactions. Their literature analysis together with their own research show that individuals are relatively good at both perceiving as well as conveying rejections, even though the rejections do not always contain the actual word 'no'. Rejections commonly entail: delays in response, prefacings (such as 'hmm' and 'well'), palliative remarks (apologies, compliments or appreciation) and accounts (explanations or justifications as to why not). Hence, rejections, in a direct verbal manner, they argue, are not easily done since, generally, rejections are not expressed in that way. Thus, rejections need to be understood in a broader manner, not necessarily through pronouncing the word 'no'.

These discussions of consent as embodied, open-ended and complex have helped me to make meaning of the young women's mixed signals. After the focus group they did give me fake phone numbers, which was an act or performance that inevitably must be considered a rejection, a non-verbal non-consent to meet up with me again. To say no, as Leila writes, 'wasn't something we could do'. As I look back, I can see that to say no in a direct manner must have been difficult, partly because, as Kitzinger and Frith (1999) argue, rejections are normally not expressed in a verbal direct manner, and partly because I did not really give them space to communicate a possible withdrawal from meeting me again. We were sitting together in a small room and had just finished an interesting focus group discussion where the young women had been very generous in their accounts. When I asked if they wanted to sign up for an interview, I remember their being vaguely affirmative, perhaps out of politeness, but not enthusiastic. I was, however, eager to interview them individually and immediately started to collect their contact details and was not receptive to, or possibly ignored, the signals of rejection I do believe were present in the room. My focus at that moment was on their narratives, especially on their accounts of *everyday racism*, rather than on them as participants. I wanted to portray their stories; however, as Back argues, there is a fine line between 'give and take in research encounters, between portrayal and betrayal' (2012, p. 24). Nevertheless, overall, their signals *were* ambivalent, as Leila also confirms in the e-mail: 'We were interested; but just then we were young, lazy girls who simply couldn't bother.' Leila's statement, besides it confirming the ambivalence that I grasped and have struggled with, indicates that consent/non-consent sometimes might be very time/context-specific: at that time, they 'simply couldn't bother'.

Moreover, I want to address the contextual circumstances that prevailed during the recruitment of participants and how these might have influenced the participants' processes of consent/non-consent. Since the selection criterion was participants between 16 and 19 years old, parental consent/consent from a legal guardian was not obtained. However, through my technique of recruiting participants, other adult figures, who sometimes are described as 'gatekeepers' (cf. Heath *et al.* 2007), in many cases were in indirect (and sometimes direct) proximity to the participants as I approached them to inform them about the project. Even though I tried to avoid these persons' direct presence by asking them to leave the space while I did so, this could have influenced the young women's decision-making in different ways. The school space, being an institutional setting, likewise could have impacted on their often affirmative first response and later withdrawal.

In the e-mail, Leila additionally, in a somewhat joking manner, wrote: '*at least I gave you the right number the second time*' followed by 'haha {*laugh*}'. Along the way, it seems, *something* made her decide to give me her correct phone number after all. Her shift is another indicator of how consent should be treated as an open-ended and non-fixed process as well as an example of how participants are active in the research process. The exact reasons for her shift are unknown to me; it could have been a decision made out of politeness or a feeling of responsibility. However, I also like to think about Leila's decision to give me the correct number the second time as connected to the discussions we had in the focus group. As mentioned earlier, at the end of the focus group Leila advised me not only to include her and her group of friends' lived experiences but also the experiences of young women who, contrary to Leila and her friends, were white and hence normatively constructed as 'Swedish'. By stating this, she used her agency to steer the research project in a direction that she believed in. If the researcher and research participant relationship, as Woodyer (2008) holds, is 'open for negotiation', it also becomes possible to recognize that participants might act against, intervene in or resist requirements set up by the researcher. They might, too, have their own reasons (even political) for *participating* in (consenting to) research (cf. Hunleth 2011, McGarry 2016). Participants, even young, such as in this case Leila, might seek to expose inequalities or tell alternative stories in order to influence the knowledge production and/or resist unequal representations, to 'talk back', to use bell hooks' phrase (1989). Leila's willingness to meet with me again could have been such an act.

What happens to consent when the interview ends?

A further important dimension to be taken into account is how the ethical principle of informed consent should be understood in connection to the progress of time. In Leila's e-mail, a link is established between *then* and *now*, as she addresses the time between the actual incidents that took place and the moment when she has read the published book. The long period of time that had passed between meeting me during the fieldwork and receiving the book had made her forget she participated in the study; thus, at first she thought the book had been mistakenly sent to her. However, as she starts to read, she also starts to remember. The progress of time is also present in Leila's explanations of what took place between us during the fieldwork. She makes a brief reference to the group's activities today and claims that what happened *then* would not have happened *now*: '*Today, we would never have done what we did back then*'. She also describes her reactions when reading my accounts of the methodological dilemmas that included her and her friends as teenagers; these, at least to some extent, I categorize as negative since it caused her feelings of shame: '*I was embarrassed when I read about it in the book*'. She is also apologetic. Leila writing to me could be understood as her taking responsibility for, or explaining, actions that in the research report actually are disconnected from her through the process of writing up the analysis and not in the least through the process of anonymization in which I changed her name to Leila, a procedure that is ethically complex too, as described by Kolankiewicz in this volume (see also Djampour 2018). However, the girl I named Leila naturally reads the text differently: she finds herself and her words in the text and she remembers, and these memories are to some extent hurtful to her. These remarks, I argue, need to be problematized in connection with what lies in the meaning and practice of informed consent. I rhetorically ask myself: When does the ethical guideline of not causing harm to participants end? What happens to consent when the interview ends and the writing of the text starts?

Trained in qualitative methods within the social sciences, I tend to arrange the research process into separate spatial and time-specific compartments: first, conducting interviews, or doing fieldwork, and second, the writing process, which often takes place at home or in the office. During the latter process, I distance myself from the material, and tendencies in the overall material at this stage of the research process become more important than individual testimonies. According to anthropologist Kristen Bell, it is during this process of writing up that the principle of informed consent, as stated by formal guidelines and ethical boards, in practice becomes challenging. She writes:

> Informed consent, as originally conceptualized, is about agreeing to be 'done to' in the context of the data collection itself. The key issue is that in ethnographic research – in any of its disciplinary formulations – for the most part, the 'doing to' doesn't happen in the fieldwork situation but, rather, in the act of writing up.
>
> (2014, p. 516)

Ethnographer Julia O'Connell Davidson, in turn, states that consenting to research is really consenting to be objectified. While the researcher moves from the field to writing, the participant, in the writing hands of the researcher, is not moving and developing with time. As the participants in their own lives, as time passes, move on, develop, change, grow and so forth, their narratives, in the research report, become an irreversible 'freeze-frame-version' of themselves (2008, p. 57). The knowledge of this, or reading a publication, O'Connell Davidson (2008) argues, could be harmful.

The 'freeze-frame-version', might be uncomfortable or, as for Leila, embarrassing when faced with it many years later. Giving more transparent information to participants about this academically taken-for-granted process where personal life stories become data would possibly diminish negative experiences of 'being done to' (Bell 2014). For Leila's part, reading about the fragments of her 16–17-year-old self in my book seems not only to have evoked negative feelings, but also more positive ones as she writes that it was fun as well as interesting to read her own words. She also writes that she was glad that I 'managed to see the positives in it all', which in my interpretation refers back to how I framed the methodological dilemmas in the book. Her e-mail is thus a mix of emotional responses deriving from her reading of the book. This duality in her response also indicates how multilayered, contradictory and emotionally mixed participating in qualitative research might be for those who agree to do this.

Concluding remarks

In this chapter, I have discussed how the implementation of the formal ethical principle of informed consent in practice, in my research project, was not a rational but a rather contradictory, open-ended process. Asking for consent might give rise to replies that shift over time or due to context, mixed or non-verbal signals or even silences. The practice of consent might also have an impact on participants beyond the actual research process: for instance, as for Leila, when faced with the researcher's interpretation of their personal interview accounts. This all, I argue, requires an overall long-term reflexive (re)thinking that not only settles with the participant's signature on the consent form but is perceptive towards ethical and methodological dilemmas, broken-off communications, silences and mixed signals that might occur throughout the process. Moreover, acknowledging the shifting power dynamics at play between researcher and research participant, during the fieldwork as well as when writing, not only might contribute to a more dynamical understanding of methodological dilemmas (such as informed consent), but could also lead to the recognition of participants as agents in the research process.

The reflexive practice of going back in time to revisit and make meaning of methodological dilemmas and discomforts of the past that I have undertaken for this chapter has been a valuable learning insight for me as a researcher. I have taken the time to reflect on, and to some extent revalue, methodological dilemmas that I was faced with during the fieldwork and how these dilemmas could be understood from a distance. Overall, I would characterize the fieldwork I conducted for this study as fragmented in the sense that interviews were often, but not always, short; scheduled interviews did not always happen; participants whom I thought I had recruited suddenly and silently, or with an excuse, withdrew themselves. Due to this, at the time of the fieldwork I undervalued my research skills, as well as the empirical material that came from it, while admiring researchers who established closer relationships with their subjects of study and thereby, I imagined, were able to hold longer and possibly richer interviews. Today I see this somewhat differently. As I have shown in this chapter, even reluctant participants who are not very talkative, who are difficult to get hold of, who speak in fragments or only when they feel like it (even 5 years later, such as Leila) have significant narratives to tell. Needless to say, my reactions to the difficulties I faced also capture the interesting relationality that exists between researchers and those we research, especially regarding how dependent researchers are on participants' consent, their acts and the quality of the empirical material that participants 'generate'.

Note

1 For further discussions on how *some* stories might require a group constellation that shares similar experiences for these experiences to be verbalized, see Sixtensson (2018).

References

Aaltonen, S., 2017. Challenges in gaining and re-gaining informed consent among young people on the margins of education. *International Journal of Social Research Methodology*, 20 (4), 329–341.

Archard, D., 1998. *Sexual Consent*. Boulder, CO: Westview.

Back, L., 2012. Live sociology: Social research and its futures. *Sociological Review*, 60 (S1), 18–39.

Bell, K., 2014. Resisting commensurability: Against informed consent as an anthropological virtue. *American Anthropologist*, 116 (3), 511–522.

Bettie, J., 2003/2014. *Women without class: Girls, race, and identity*. Berkeley: University of California Press.

CODEX, rules & guidelines for research, 2020. *Informed Consent*. Available from: http://www.codex.vr.se/en/manniska2.shtml [Accessed 27 August 2020].

Djampour, P., 2018. *Borders crossing bodies: The stories of eight youths with experience of migrating*. Thesis (PhD). Malmö University.

Gallagher, M., Haywood, S.L., Jones, M.W. and Milne, S., 2010. Negotiating informed consent with children in school-based research: A critical review. *Children & Society*, 24 (6), 471–482.

Gunnarsson, L., 2020. *Samtyckesdynamiker: Sex, våldtäkt och gråzonen däremellan [Consent dynamics: Sex, rape and the grey area in between]*. Lund: Studentlitteratur.

Heath, S., Charles, V., Crow, G. and Wiles, R., 2007. Informed consent, gatekeepers and go-betweens: Negotiating consent in child and youth-orientated institutions. *British Educational Research Journal*, 33 (3), 403–417.

Hickman, S.E. and Muehlenhard, C.L., 1999. 'By the semi-mystical appearance of a condom': How young women and men communicate sexual consent in heterosexual situations. *Journal of Sex Research*, 36 (3), 258–272.

Holt, L., 2004. The 'voices' of children: De-centring empowering research relations. *Children's Geographies*, 2 (1), 13–27.

hooks, b., 1989. *Talking back: Thinking feminist, thinking black*. Boston, MA: South End Press.

Hunleth, J., 2011. Beyond *on* or *with*: Questioning power dynamics and knowledge production in 'child-oriented' research methodology. *Childhood*, 18 (1), 81–93.

Kitzinger, C. and Frith, H., 1999. Just Say No? The use of Conversation Analysis in developing a feminist perspective on sexual refusal. *Discourse & Society*, 10 (3), 293–316.

McGarry, O., 2016. Repositioning the research encounter: Exploring power dynamics and positionality in youth research. *International Journal of Social Research Methodology*, 19 (3), 339–354.

O'Connell Davidson, J., 2008. If no means no, does yes mean yes? Consenting to research intimacies. *History of the Human Sciences*, 21 (4), 49–67.

Sixtensson, J., 2018. *Härifrån till framtiden. Om gränslinjer, aktörskap och motstånd i tjejers vardagsliv [From here to the future. On boundaries, actors and resistance in girls' everyday lives]*. Thesis (PhD). Malmö University.

Skelton, T., 2008. Research with children and young people: Exploring the tensions between ethics, competence and participation. *Children's Geographies*, 6 (1), 21–36.

Woodyer, T., 2008. The body as research tool: Embodied practice and children's geographies. *Children's Geographies*, 6 (4), 349–362.

3

CREATING KNOWLEDGE THROUGH COMMUNITY THEATRE

No Border Musical and the making of representations

Emma Söderman

> When I started to participate in the *No Border Musical*, I was hidden [*gömd*], so it was a bit difficult for me to go out and be visible, but then I thought that I must be visible and show that this is unfair and, yeah, and then I thought that it is important to be in this musical and inform people [about the situation for undocumented people].
>
> (Nima, panel discussion, 09.11.2013)

In this quote from a panel discussion after a performance of the *No Border Musical*, Nima, who was an actor in the performance, puts forward that due to residing as an undocumented migrant with an overhanging threat of expulsion, he was supposed to be invisible. Nima had contested this invisibility by entering on stage, thus making himself visible in public. Initiated by activists in the local migrant rights movement in Malmö, Sweden, the *No Border Musical* was created in 2011 and continued until 2013. The ensemble was constituted by people linked to the migrant rights movement; about half of the participants resided as undocumented during parts of the 2-year period of working together in the ensemble. Those residing as undocumented had sought asylum in Sweden as unaccompanied minors, but had received a decision of expulsion due to the Dublin II Regulation.[1] One important motivation for the *No Border Musical* was to illustrate the consequences of restrictive asylum policies and violent migration control. Immersed in the context of the local migrant rights movement, while critically addressing inequalities, the creation of the musical performance shares characteristics with theatre practices commonly described as 'community theatre' (van Erven 2001).

My aim in this chapter is to analyze the making of the *No Border Musical*, from the perspective of a *politics of representation*, meaning that I analyze how specific practices of representation play out in a particular time and place (Hall 1997; see also Introduction in this volume), in this case a community theatre in a context of migration control and the migrant rights movement in Sweden. I address the politics of representation through an analysis of the relationships between the stories performed on stage and the actors' own biographies, the contestation of invisibility connected to migration status, as well as through exploring the absences in the making of the musical's performance of representations of experiences of migration. Absences in this chapter work as an entry point to discuss some aspects of tensions in the making of representations. Furthermore, community theatre as a way of explicitly working with experiences and representation may also give new insight to the politics of representation played out in practical and performative work (cf. Kaptani and Yuval-Davis 2008).

The following chapter is a reflection on the methodology used in the study *Resistance through acting: Ambivalent practices of the No Border Musical* (Söderman 2019). It was an ethnography of the musical in which I participated as a researcher as well as a non-professional actor with a background in migrant rights activism. Besides having taken part in the processes I study, I had thus also been engaged in the larger context of migrant rights activism within which the musical took place. This methodological entry point can be referred to as 'activist research' (Hale 2008), which I address further below.

Before discussing activist research, I continue with a section situating the chapter in relation to discussions within research on theatre, specifically different forms of participatory theatre. I furthermore provide a short description on the content of the *No Border Musical*'s performance, followed by the analytical parts of the chapter where I discuss different tensions in relation to the musical's working process of creating representations of migration control. I conclude the chapter with some suggestions on how activist research and community theatre as research method can provide in-depth knowledge concerning how the politics of representation is played out in practice.

Theatre and the politics of representation

As I mentioned in the introduction, the *No Border Musical* could be understood as community theatre. Community theatre, as a form of collaborative performance and working process of theatre production, can be traced back to various forms of countercultural, radical, anti- and post-colonial, educational and liberational theatres of the 1960s and 1970s (van Erven 2001). Today, the combination of artistic and political practices in theatre production has many names: community theatre, community-based theatre, grassroots theatre, theatre for social change, social theatre, applied theatre, etc. The Brazilian writer and theatre director Augusto Boal has been very influential in the field of community theatre with his work on the theatre of the oppressed (Boal 1979), where theatre is understood as a form of 'rehearsal' for revolution. Community theatre connects to political and popular theatre in the sense of trying to create platforms for addressing political issues. Furthermore, community theatre also aims for a collaborative working process including people living in communities affected by issues addressed in the performance (Salverson 2011). The aim of creating the *No Border Musical*, in a context of borders and violent control of migration, was to make visible the consequences these processes have for individuals in need of protection. The musical thus combined aesthetic expression and a collaborative working process, with an ambition to transform the present society.

One underlying assumption about the work of the musical seems to be that increased 'approval' of refugees will come from facing them and gaining knowledge of their experiences as refugees. Within the field of participatory theatre, this is a common assumption, which can be connected to Levinas' ideas of 'the face' (Thompson 2011). In the meeting with the face of the other, Levinas traces an actualization of an ethical responsibility, combined with a realization that we cannot fully know the other. Inspired by Levinas, theatre scholar Thompson writes: 'the face can be conceived of as having a force that operates at the level of affect, and one that suggests, or makes us feel, the restriction in our capacity for understanding' (Thompson 2011, p. 162). In regard to the assumption of affect when meeting the face of the other, creating a theatre about bordering and migration control together with actors having experiences of these issues, in a context of the asylum system and of provision of refuge to refugees, is still a balancing act. For example, there is a risk of reproducing a rather violent 'imperative to tell' (Thompson 2011, pp. 56 ff.) to prove oneself worthy of receiving protection within the state. Participatory theatre is argued to 'tread a precarious line between producing validation, on the one hand, and victimhood, on the other' (Jeffers 2008, p. 217).

Theatre can, furthermore, in itself be understood as a space of transformation, of boundlessness, where the actors are at least temporarily transformed by acting in character and where there is potential for the audience to be transformed by the performance (Wittrock 2011). The artists on stage acting in character are not themselves, at the same time as they are not *not* themselves (Schechner 1985). In other words, the audience will read the actor through notions of what the looks and actions of the actor signal to them, in combination with the character performed by the actor (Wittrock 2011). In a context of theatre performances addressing issues of asylum and refugees, theatre scholar Caroline Wake uses the concept of *faceness* to capture the conflation between the actor and the character: 'Faceness refers to the vague and generalized humanity that an audience grants asylum seekers when they see a face that looks – to them, at least – like what an asylum seeker's face might look like' (Wake 2013, p. 113). Wake uses the concept of faceness to analyze the phenomenon of actors acting as someone else, but at the same time being cast due to their personal (in contrast to professional) biography, as well as actors acting as themselves.

Together, the ensemble created a performance addressing experiences of migration control and asylum processes, where some of the actors could also be read by the audience as carriers of these experiences; thus, fruitful for exploring how the politics of representation is played out in practical and performative work. As I will discuss below, the musical could be understood to blur and/or fuse the relation between the biography of the actors with experiences of migration control and the characters illustrating similar hardships on stage. Before proceeding with the analysis, I provide a short note on my role as a researcher and participant in the musical.

A short note on activist research

If theatre in general, and community theatre in particular, could be understood as boundless or as boundary-crossing, in terms of transformation of character/actor/audience, and in terms of crossing boundaries of politics and art, then this chapter could also be seen as resting on yet another crossing of academic work, activism and art. My fieldwork was thus, for me, not just a time for collecting the material for my thesis. I was part of the ensemble and, during the approximately 2 years of working with the musical, it was a large part of my everyday life. I shared an apartment with participants in the musical, met participants when we rehearsed and performed, or in the streets, over a cup of coffee, for interviews, etc. Some participants in the musical were already friends of mine, as we had worked together in the local migrant rights group prior to joining the ensemble, and other participants became my friends and interlocutors during the process of creating the performance. The overall context to which I and the musical belong/ed can be described as a network of friends, activists and acquaintances who in one way or another are involved in or sympathize with political organizing, seeking to transform injustices in society, including injustices facing people subject to violent migration control. The academic research was integrated into this context and its point of entry was an insight that academia is yet another arena in which the struggles against injustices can and need to take place through knowledge production. Representing and analyzing processes and practices of the *No Border Musical* was one such project.

Frequently grounded in feminist epistemologies, the combination of academic work and political involvement has sometimes been called 'activist research' (Hale 2008). It is related to the praxis of critical ethnography as it often involves creating knowledge setting out from some kind of participation in the communities and issues being studied. The musical was a forum for dialogues, struggles and knowledge creation around some of the pressing issues of our time, such as asylum, migration, belonging, recognition, injustice, redistribution and borders, played out in specific ways according to the times and locations of the performances. From my experiences of working with the musical, I suggest that the boundaries between the knowledge created within academia and the knowledge created through activism need to be questioned (see also Chesters 2012). I further suggest that theatre as part of methodology can provide possibilities to create new knowledge (cf. Kaptani and Yuval-Davis 2008): in this chapter, knowledge about the politics of representation played out in practice in the context of community theatre and migration control. The musical's working process and performances formed a 'possibility of radical perspective from which to see and create, to imagine alternatives, new worlds' (hooks 2004, p. 157), simultaneously also being permeated by dividing lines connected to precarious legal status.

Warm-up before one of the earliest shorter performances by the *No Border Musical*. Photograph: Amelie Herbertsson.

The musical performance included stories of experiences of migration and seeking asylum in Europe, as well as addressed questions of who enjoys the privilege of travelling without constraints. It also illustrated a utopian world without borders where people themselves would be able to choose which locations to call home. The scenography was simple, with black boxes being moved around to represent borders, tables or a podium for speakers during a political rally. To portray the shift between a no-borders future/present, and a bordering present/past, different lighting, music and textiles were used.

The overarching narrative of the musical performance patchwork was situated in the future, where the characters met to celebrate the anniversary of the abolition of nation-state borders. Through the different characters, the audience was then shown how things used to look when borders sorted, differentiated and separated people. The audience met characters working for the Swedish Migration Agency, characters residing as undocumented, and characters who were charged in court due to helping detainees to escape. The performance also told stories of how the borders were abolished, and how numerous small acts of resistance together overthrew the system. The performance lasted for about 1 hour and 40 minutes. The musical was performed in Malmö, Norrköping and Stockholm during 2012–2013.

No Border Musical
en gränslös föreställning
soo bandhigid aan xuduud lahayn

خت ی ل ن ودب ن مرز

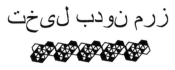

First page of the programme distributed when the musical was performed. Illustration: Sofie Persson

Experiences of migration control on stage

The musical's script was based on stories gathered from persons connected to the local migrant rights movement, but not necessarily participants of the ensemble, drawing on their experiences as asylum-seekers, undocumented persons and/or engaged in migrant rights issues. Thus, whilst the performance was aimed at making experiences of migration control and the violence of borders visible, it did not claim to represent any of the actors' *personal* experiences of seeking asylum. At the same time, the actors with experiences of seeking asylum and residing as undocumented were not *not* performing their experiences, either in relation to how they were viewed by the audience or other participants, or in relation to how they themselves talked about the performance.

> When I first came to the musical, I didn't know what it was all about. Then I realized that the story was about Jawad [a character on stage]. That it was about a life very similar to my own. So, I thought, it's good to participate and perform in front of people because this is my life too.
>
> (Alireza, interview, 09.10.2012)

This is my life too, says Alireza, thus highlighting that, although he had not shared his personal experiences as a starting point for writing the musical's script, he felt that what he was performing on stage was similar to what he had experienced as a migrant seeking refuge. That some of the actors had experiences similar to those performed on stage was also highlighted by participants without personal experiences of migration control:

> I think that it [the musical] gave a voice and face to the people who have gone through this, that it's super-important for all these stories and experiences to be given a voice and identity, and not just a sad identity but one that perhaps has experienced nice things or perhaps is both angry and happy, frightened and brave and so on.
>
> (Lena, group interview, 28.09.2015)

What Alireza and Lena are each talking about, although from different positions, is the idea that to be face-to-face with the other opens up possibilities for a deepened understanding of the other (Thompson 2011). At the same time, the other is irreducible to the representation of the face (Burggraeve 1999). Partly, this is what Lena is talking about: through the process of creating a theatre about migration control and bordering practices, the other has been made visible to her in more complex forms (as 'angry and happy, frightened and brave'), and she thinks that this more 'full' or 'complex' face of the other might be visible in the musical's performance as well. To this discussion, the concept of faceness adds a caution that when a person racialized as brown/black performs experiences of migration control on stage, independent of whether their personal biography accords with those experiences, the actor is understood as, and maybe also limited to, being a carrier of the experiences of flight, bordering and migration control (see Wake 2013). As Lena said, this was partly the purpose: to provide these experiences of seeking asylum, and of migration control, with a face, a face that would signal a more complex human being than would appear when limited to viewing people only through categories of asylum-seeker or refugee. This makes visible a tension: on the one hand, to use a category, or experiences, as a point of departure for political mobilization to make visible what mainstream society has not acknowledged; on the other hand, the risk of reproducing the very category one aims to dismantle.[2]

In relation to racism specifically, Burggraeve (1999), building on Levinas, argues that:

> the core of racism consists not in the denial of, or the failure to appreciate, similarities between people, but in the denial of, or better said, failure to appreciate and value, people's differences, or better still, the fundamental and irreducible otherness by which they fall outside of every genre and are thus 'unique'.
>
> (Burggraeve, p. 40)

That is, unique in the sense that they are not possible to fit into any given category, or to be given any specific label. The point of departure for the participants of the musical was that in the act of highlighting experiences of bordering practices, partly through having actors with these experiences on stage, a critique of the migration regime was included. Simultaneously, this type of mobilization seems to carry a danger of saying that, 'Look, even though they are refugees, they are like us (they can be happy, brave, sad etc.).' Furthermore, besides a couple of exceptions, the whole musical was in Swedish, which could be understood as a way to communicate to a (Swedish) audience that, 'Look, they [refugees] are like us [Swedes] as they can speak Swedish.' By only viewing the performance and not knowing anything about its context, this analysis could certainly be put forward. Through my participation in the working process of the musical, however, I know that it leaves out some important aspects. Performing experiences of migration control on stage can be put in contrast to the experiences of being made invisible in society, as one participant said about residing undocumented: 'It felt as if I was far away from society' (Alireza, interview, 9 October 2012). The seriousness of this experience, of being 'far from society' or being made invisible, has been emphasized by research concerned with undocumented persons in a Swedish context (Sager 2011, 2018). Sager highlights the fear of being unseen, at the same time as one fears being seen, in the sense of being detected as undocumented (Sager 2011, 2018).

The participants in the musical who resided as undocumented with an over-hanging threat of being expelled all expressed fear as a constant companion in their everyday life. Fear of being detected as undocumented affected how they moved around in the city, their mental and physical health, how they made contact with new people, and of course also the work of the musical. During the 2 years of working together, the issue of safety for participants residing as undocumented was discussed continuously and different measures were taken to decrease risks of detection. The fear of participants being detected as undocumented also affected my entry point for understanding the experiences of performing on stage for those residing as undocumented, where I thought that performing would necessarily be intertwined with strong feelings of fear. Contrary to what I had expected, Nima, upon my question about how he had experienced standing on stage as undocumented, answered:

> When I was on stage, I did not even think of the police or that I'm undocumented. I just felt that I'm part of a musical and I'm on stage and I'm going to perform well.
>
> (Nima, interview, 15.04.2014)

The first quote in this chapter was also from Nima, where he said that he had felt a need to be visible and to inform others about the situation of undocumented people in Sweden. Through performing different stories related to experiences of migration control and bordering practices, the musical sought to create knowledge and, through knowledge, change in the migration regime. The stories told in the musical were understood in relation to what the actors signalled to the audience through their bodily appearance, and the actors themselves also talked about the stories performed in relation to their own experiences of migration control, or as a way to give these experiences a 'face'. However, as Nima's quote points to, performing in the musical was also about being part of a theatre group and of doing well when on stage, of creating a good performance.

'Right kind' of visibility

Migrant protests often involve struggles to be visible and audible; at the same time, making oneself visible includes a risk of being subject to migration control (Tyler and Marciniak 2013). Although the point of departure is the situation of undocumented individuals, Sager (2016, 2018) argues that the tension between invisibility and visibility in the Swedish context is not limited to the category of undocumented, but also concerns people subject to racialization in general. Critical post-colonial and antiracist research has brought to light that 'the approach of the Swedish welfare institutions towards racialised citizens and residents, as well as political debates on issues such as migration, racism, discrimination and colonialism, is characterised by an interaction between invisibility and hypervisibility' (Sager 2018, p. 176). The experiences of racism of groups subject to racialization are not acknowledged and those groups are denied representation as part of Sweden in the labour market and in the social and cultural spheres – and are thus made invisible. At the same time, these groups are subject to hypervisibility, where they are represented through images of criminalization, victimization, pathologization and stigmatization in general. Quoting Lacatus, Sager highlights that: 'Sociocultural visibility is a process, a continuous and dynamic negotiation for the right kind of exposure' (Lacatus 2008, p. 125, cited in Sager 2016, p. 118). The musical could be seen as a negotiation of the 'right kind' of exposure and visibility and as providing a chance to choose an arena from where to be seen, from where to speak, as well as what subjects, and from which angles, to address.

One text in the musical's script was written by a person who had been deported from Sweden to Afghanistan. He was never part of the ensemble but contributed by writing this poem, which was then reworked into a song in the performance. His words travelled from Afghanistan to Sweden. Traces of this travel remained in the text: there was sometimes an absence of the letters å, ä and ö (it was written in Swedish) and he occasionally included an explanation of pieces of text inside brackets. For example, after the sentence 'thunderstorms cause terror now in skies that are quite clear', he wrote '(thunderstorms in clear skies are bombs dropped in Afghanistan, last week 87 died in my hometown)'.

This poem is a story beginning with his experiences of residing as undocumented in Sweden, of being detected, put in a detention centre and then deported. His voice was clearly not supposed to be heard or represented in public. By being detained and deported from Swedish territory, he had been made into a mere commodity to be stored (detention centre, *förvar* in Swedish, translates as 'storage' or 'warehouse') and transported. However, his words travelled to Sweden – first to Malmö and, eventually, all the way to the Young Royal Dramatic Theatre[3] in Stockholm. While it did not change the fact that he had been deported, it did contest the act of deportation as an act of silencing and of making invisible. The poem he wrote that became a song in the musical was called *Sick system*:

I travelled over half the earth
asking for no more than a little peace
the pens in their hands were like knives and they made red crosses at my name
Refrain: I got lost on streets that lay in darkness the sun was shining but I cast
no shadow the system is sick
thunderstorms cause terror now in skies that are quite clear (thunderstorms in
clear skies are bombs dropped in Afghanistan, last week 87 died in my home
town)
straight roads are like mountains that have to be climbed
I was not cold behind doors that were closed
but felt the chill of their hearts that were cold
handcuffs and cells have made me disappear
what will they do now? for I will not stop fighting

Refrain
faked smiles and bent words on paper disappoint
(the Migration Agency uses strange language in its letters, they say one thing
and mean something else)
I knew that all they wanted was to play
how can human beings be illegal
I don't understand, can someone explain
they block the way between the doctor and the sick
can someone tell me how much lower they can sink

Refrain
sometimes I just want to let go of it all
I got tired, the pressure was too great
some fine people came and taught me a lesson, my fate is for myself alone to
decide,
now I want to reach out my hand for the others for that's my only way to
avenge

These words were read on stage in a spoken-word style by four actors (two sharing the author's experiences of residing as undocumented in Sweden and two actors without these experiences), and a choir of actors sang the refrain in between each verse. In the refrain, 'the sun was shining but I cast no shadow' may be interpreted as referring to the existential dimension of being made invisible in relation to the experience of residing as undocumented. In this sense, to have the experiences as undocumented represented on stage can be understood as a contestation of being made invisible, of being non-represented (or of being represented in 'wrong' ways, as a criminal for example). Furthermore, the poem does not end with the deportation. Instead, it ends with a desire to avenge. And this desire is formulated as an act of solidarity: 'Some fine people came and taught me a lesson, my fate is for myself alone to decide, now I want to reach out my hand for the others for that's my only way to avenge'.

In the song, there is resistance against the condition of being undocumented and there is also a rising-up and an aim to avenge. Another form of visibility, breaking with the limitations of invisibility or hypervisibility, is created in this song. The poem may be viewed as a process of struggling for the right kind of visibility, where the poem addresses invisibility ('no shadow') and hypervisibility (being criminalized through detention and deportation) but ends with a form of visibility that is rebellious and based on solidarity.

Tensions in the making of representations

Besides the poem/song referred to above, the musical performance included rewritten versions of popular songs, as well as lyrics and songs written by the musical's participants themselves. These varied in style and included punk, rap, spoken word, electro and singer-songwriter. The musical genres may be linked to the milieu of activism from which the *No Border Musical* grew, and the songs from the musical have also been sung at a number of protests and demonstrations after it was performed. Absent from the performance were music and songs originating from the countries (Afghanistan, Iran, Somalia and Palestine) where some of the ensemble had grown up. This absence points to some of the tensions in terms of the making of representations in the musical; added to that, the process of making some stories or experiences visible always carries the risk of unintentionally contributing to other issues staying invisible (Fernandes 2017).

Considering which characters were played by whom, it seems as though it was easier for actors with personal experiences of migration control to cross over and play, for example, the head of the Migration Agency, police officers and prosecutor, than for actors without such experiences to cross over and stage experiences of flight and separation. This happened only once, with two undocumented characters, where the focus was more on resistance than on the suffering produced by violent migration control.

All actors with bodily appearance who could be read as performing their personal experiences of migration control were young men from Somalia and Afghanistan (except for a woman who joined later in the process), a reflection of the contact net of the local migrant rights group at the time. Besides the young male actors with experiences of flight, the majority of the rest of the ensemble were white women/queers in their 25s–35s. Despite this rather specific composition of the ensemble, the different bodily appearances of the actors in terms of perceptions of gender, race and/or nationality were hardly ever brought up in the ensemble.

One exception was when the young woman, who was part of the ensemble in its later stages, pointed out in a panel discussion after a performance that, before she joined, there were no women with experiences of migration control in the group:

> 'where are all the undocumented women?' I mean, they are here in Sweden; I know that they exist. I'm proof of that! But where are they? Why are they not seen or heard?
>
> (Salam, panel discussion, 09.11.2013)

Furthermore, I recall only once that the issue of how the audience would perceive the characters in terms of race was discussed in the ensemble. A participant with experiences of residing as undocumented said, when we were recreating a scene of a deportation and border control, that it might not be clear to the audience what would be happening on stage, as the actors playing the roles of the border guards had 'black' and not 'yellow' hair. In the end, it was decided not to change the casting to a border guard with 'yellow' hair because the content of the scene was presumed to be sufficiently clear without such a change.

Although not explicitly voiced by the participants, this discussion is closely related to the 'faceness' of the actors. An actor signalling a personal biography of flight and migration control to the audience was perceived to be less suitable for playing the role of a border guard, whereas an actor perceived as white was presumed to provide a clearer picture of a border guard in the story told on stage. A white body was thus assumed to represent violent border controls in a clearer manner. Both Salam's critique and the rehearsal of this scene shed light, as mentioned, on the fact that the actors with experiences of migration control, when playing certain characters, both understood themselves and were read as revealing their personal experiences, although the script was not based on these. Nonetheless, how the roles were distributed between the different actors was not subject to any in-depth discussions with the whole ensemble. At the same time, there seemed to have been an assumption related to the bodily appearance of the actors with experiences of flight and migration control, as can be inferred from the quote above, of giving these experiences a 'face'. During the working process, however, there was silence around what the bodily appearance of the actors meant for the performance, both in terms of gender and race.

The absence of discussions on matters of the different bodily appearances of the actors on stage can be put in relation to issues of representation within the migrant rights movement. In Sweden, the migrant rights movement was founded in the 1980s, in a context marked by restrictive migration reforms and racist and antiracist mobilizations (Jämte 2013). According to a governmental study from 1999, the migrant rights movement (termed '*flyktinggömmarna*' [refugee hiders] in the study) was part of a new generation of movements in Sweden, linked to the broader antiracist movement. The early migrant rights movement has generally involved individuals born in Sweden who, due to religious beliefs or political conviction and/or due to encounters with rejected asylum–seekers, have chosen to act (SOU 1999, Rosengren 2009). Although not all participants in the musical had a background of involvement in the migrant rights movement, a majority of the participants without experiences of migration control took part in activities and/or were in different ways engaged in the milieu of extra-parliamentary activism. Contemporaneous with the period when the musical was active, there were ongoing discussions in the local migrant rights movement and its wider extra-parliamentary leftist context about who was perceived as an 'activist' and what this label entailed. These discussions also included problematizing the experienced homogeneity and whiteness of the activist scene. The migrant rights movement in this context stood out as it involved more people with a migrant background themselves, most of whom were women/queers (Hansen 2019). In the ensemble, however, a vast majority of those with a background in the migrant rights movement or extra-parliamentary left were women/queers without personal experiences of racism and/or migration control. The idea behind the musical also came from activists without any direct experiences of seeking asylum or being subject to migration control; even so, partly as a consequence of being situated in a migrant rights movement where discussions linked to issues of representation were on the agenda, the ensemble came to be constituted both by people with experiences of residing as undocumented and by people without these experiences. Yet, despite the discussion on representation within the migrant rights movement growing during the period the ensemble was working together,[4] the issue of representation in terms of how the actors would be read by the audience with regard to, for example, gender, nationality or race was not something discussed to any great extent during the working process of the musical. When it was discussed, it focused on the risks of being detected and arrested for those who could be read as undocumented.[5]

I suggest that the absence of discussions in the musical around how different actors would be perceived by the audience may be related to the fact that the migrant rights movement, at least previously, has often prioritized problems of racism in relation to state practices of migration control – maybe at the expense of engaging in questions about the risk of reproducing problematic representations through the practices within the movement. Further, in relation to risks of detection and deportation, self-representation may have been perceived as too risky in many situations. The ambition to assess and prevent the risk of participants being detected as undocumented was a central issue during the musical's working process. Furthermore, for the individuals risking deportation, contesting this expulsion may be articulated as the first priority, and the focus of the migrant rights movement on repressive state practices (instead of on internal representation) may be understood as a response to this priority as well. Nonetheless, I do still find it remarkable that, during the period that the ensemble (including myself) was working and performing together, issues of representation, or the relation between character and actor, were not raised in any in-depth discussion.

Conclusion

> Thank you for seeing me, when the law forced me to be invisible
> Thank you for daring to be visible, despite it being dangerous
>
> (Script, *No Border Musical*)

This quote pinpoints a central aspect of the work of the musical: of highlighting experiences of migration control and of residing as undocumented in Sweden. Fear in relation to those actors residing as undocumented being detected by the police was present throughout the work of the musical, and the above quote is part of a scene that formulates both the act of making oneself visible and of seeing the person made visible, as acts part of an abolition of borders.

I started this chapter by suggesting that the musical performance and its making illuminated a politics of representation, understood as the relation between the actor's biography and the character they played, contestation of invisibility connected to residing as undocumented, and tensions in the making of representations of migration control. I also suggested that community theatre as part of a methodological point of entry could give new insights into how the politics of representation is managed in practice. Analyzing the matter of making representations of migration control in the context of the musical showed that one issue of representation, that of being made visible as undocumented on stage, as in the quote above, was continuously addressed in the musical's work. This, while discussions on the issue of perceptions of the bodily appearances of the actors in terms of gender, race and/or nationality, to a large extent were absent, which I understand to have been connected to challenges of representation in political struggles, specifically the migrant rights movement.

Community theatre as method in my case provided an analytical angle that could move beyond seeing the work of the musical only within the framework of a violent imperative to tell in order to be accepted as a refugee, to valuing the work of the musical in terms of contesting the existential dimension of invisibility connected to residing as undocumented in Sweden. It also provided an in-depth knowledge about how the script and the performance were created, including those aspects of representation that were absent from the process of creating the performance. My background in the local migrant rights movement and my participation in creating the musical performance, simultaneously with doing fieldwork for my thesis, gave insight into the complexities and difficulties of activism through community theatre, here analyzed in relation to the politics of representation, an analysis which I suggest is relevant both for an academic and an activist audience. This because methodological questions and activism involve not only 'premises about truth and how it may be known and understood', but as important also is '*how* one goes about acquiring that knowledge' (De Genova 2005, p. 21, *italics in original*). At a time when bordering practices become ever more violent and far-reaching, researchers engage in struggles setting out from a common ground (in this case, to participate in creating a performance), and may contribute to the issues at hand, whilst also contributing to discussions about the complexities and difficulties of practices of solidarity in precarious settings. Finally, it may also spark possibilities of imagining and creating alternatives.

The pain experienced as a consequence of strict migration control and racism is severe, and to focus on how this can be resisted, how alternatives can be created, as well as visions for another world, are as important now as when the musical was performed. Sweden follows the European (and the rich parts of the world in general) trend to pour money and resources into practices of detention, deportation and border control. Furthermore, not only migrants are criminalized but those in solidarity with migrants also face criminalization, which might make the support and political work for migrant rights even more difficult. The solidarities that can be created in this context are precarious, probably temporary and need to adapt to a rapidly changing landscape of racism and migration control. A fundamental concern is, of course, to be cautious about how these solidarities might also reproduce aspects of the same structures of oppression that they aim to dismantle. Meanwhile, to work towards their creation, and prolonged presence, even if inchoate, is of utmost importance. I'll give the final words to the musical:

Initiating fight mode
All passports in the sea
There's a new time ahead of us
Where we'll all be free
(Song, 'Nations are bad for you', *No Border Musical*)

Notes

1 The Dublin II Regulation is a binding measure of European Community law, which stipulates that the first EU country to which the asylum-seeker arrives is responsible for processing the application. If the asylum-seeker seeks asylum in another EU country, he/she will in most cases (there are exceptions to this rule; however, they are applied restrictively in Sweden) be deported back to the first country of arrival. Signed by Sweden in 1995, the Dublin Convention was replaced by the **Dublin II Regulation** in 2003; that Regulation was in turn replaced by the **Dublin III Regulation** in 2013. The participants in the musical fell under the jurisdiction of the Dublin II Regulation.

2 This is by no means a new discussion but has, for example, been part of the feminist movement and the mobilization, as well as theoretization, setting out from 'women's' experiences (Mulinari and Sandell 1999).

3 Two of the last performances of the musical were staged at the reputable venue of the Young Royal Dramatic Theatre in Stockholm, where theatre intended to attract a younger audience is created.

4 This was also related to mobilizations initiated by young people in Malmö, who themselves had experiences of coming to Sweden and seeking asylum (see Djampour and Söderman 2016).

5 During the period of working with the musical, Malmö was part of a pilot project (REVA) for making deportations from Sweden more effective. Partly due to this project, there were numerous ID controls carried out by the police in the streets. Generally, in recent years the police have also received ever-increasing resources to carry out internal control of foreigners (Arena idé 2014 [Arena Think-Tank 2014] and Rikspolisstyrelsen 2009–2012 [the National Police Board 2009–2012]).

References

Arena Idé, 2014. *Skyldig tills motsats bevisats? En granskning av polisens inre utlänningskontroller [Guilty until proven otherwise? An examination of the police's internal aliens checks]. Arenagruppen.* Available from: http://arenaide.se/rapporter/skyldig-tills-motsatsen-bevisats/ [Accessed 13 January 2019].

Boal, A., 1979. *Theater of the oppressed.* London: Pluto Press.

Burggraeve, R., 1999. Violence and the vulnerable face of the other: The vision of Emmanuel Levinas on moral evil and our responsibility. *Journal of Social Philosophy*, 30 (1), 29–45.

Chesters, G., 2012. Social movements and the ethics of knowledge production. Social Movement Studies. *Journal of Social, Cultural and Political Protest*, 11 (2), 145–160.

De Genova, N. 2005. *Working the boundaries: Race, space, and "illegality" in Mexican Chicago.* Durham: Duke University Press.

Djampour, P. and Söderman, E. 2016. Att göra politik: Asylstafetten och No Border Musical [Making politics: The asylum relay and the No Border Musical]. In: M. Sager, H. Holgersson and K. Öberg, eds. *Irreguljär migration i Sverige: Rättigheter, vardagserfarenheter, motstånd och statliga kategoriseringar [Irregular migration in Sweden: Rights, everyday experiences, resistance and government categorizations].* Göteborg: Daidalos.

Fernandes, S., 2017. *Curated stories: The uses and misuses of storytelling.* Oxford Scholarship online. Available from: https://oxford.universitypressscholarship.com/view/10.1093/acprof:oso/9780190618049.001.0001/acprof-9780190618049.

Hale, R.C., ed., 2008. *Engaging contradictions: Theory, politics, and methods of activist scholarship.* Berkeley, CA; Los Angeles, CA: University of California Press.

Hall, S., ed., 1997. *Representation: Cultural representation and signifying practices.* London; California; New Delhi: SAGE.

Hansen, C., 2019. *Solidarity in diversity. Activism as pathway of migrant emplacement in Malmö.* Thesis (PhD). Malmö University.

hooks, b., 2004. Choosing the margin as a space for radical openness. In: S. Harding, ed. *The Feminist Standpoint Theory Reader.* London: Routledge.

Jämte, J., 2013. *Antirasismens många ansikten.* Thesis (PhD) Umeå: Umeå University.

Jeffers, A., 2008. Dirty truth: Personal narrative, victimhood and participatory theatre work with people seeking asylum. *Research in Drama Education*, 13 (2), 217–221.

Kaptani, E. and Yuval-Davis, N., 2008. Participatory theatre as methodology: Identity, performance and social action among refugees. *Sociological Research Online*, 13 (5).

Mulinari, D. and Sandell, K., 1999. Exploring the notion of experience in feminist thought. *Acta Sociologica*, 42 (4), 287–297.

Rikspolisstyrelsen, 2009–2012. Regleringsbrev [Regulation letter]. Available from: https://www.esv.se/statsliggaren/regleringsbrev/?RBID=11057 (2009). https://www.esv.se/statsliggaren/regleringsbrev/?RBID=12483 (2010). https://www.esv.se/statsliggaren/regleringsbrev/?RBID=13091 (2011). https://www.esv.se/statsliggaren/regleringsbrev/?RBID=13965 (2012).

Rosengren, A., 2009. *Vinna eller försvinna – om flykt, asyl och hjälpare [Win or disappear – about escape, asylum and helpers].* Stockholm: Carlssons Bokförlag.

Sager, M., 2011. *Everyday clandestinity. Experiences on the margins of citizenship and migration policies.* Thesis (PhD). Lund University.

Sager, M., 2016. Papperslöshetens o/synlighet i vardag, politik och debatt. debatt [The paperlessness/visibility in everyday life, politics and debate]. In: M. Sager, H. Holgersson and K. Öberg, eds. *Irreguljär Migration i Sverige. Rättigheter, vardagserfarenheter, motstånd och statliga kategoriseringar [Irregular migration in Sweden. Rights, everyday experiences, resistance and government categorizations].* Göteborg: Daidalos.

Sager, M., 2018. Struggles around representation and in/visibility in everyday migrant irregularity in Sweden. *Nordic Journal of Migration Research*, 8 (3), 175–182.

Salverson, J., ed., 2011. *Community engaged theatre and performance.* Toronto: Playwrights Canada Press.

Schechner, R., 1985. *Between theater & anthropology* [Electronic resource]. Philadelphia: University of Pennsylvania Press.

SOU 1999:101 *Olydiga medborgare? [Disobedient citizens?].* Available from: https://www.riksdagen.se/sv/dokument-lagar/dokument/statens-offentliga- utredningar/sou-1999-101-_GNB3101 [Accessed: 13 January 2019].

Söderman, E., 2019. *Resistance through acting: Ambivalent practices of the No Border Musical.* Thesis (PhD). Lund University.

Thompson, J., 2011. *Performance affects: Applied theatre and the end of effect.* Basingstoke: Palgrave Macmillan.

Tyler, I. and Marciniak, K., 2013. Immigrant protest: An introduction. *Citizenship Studies*, 17 (2), 143–156.

Van Erven, E., 2001. *Community theatre: Global perspectives.* London: Routledge.

Wake, C., 2013. To witness mimesis: The politics, ethics, and aesthetics of testimonial theatre in Through the Wire'. *Modern Drama*, 56 (1), 102–125.

Wittrock, H., 2011. *Säg inte mötesplats! Teater och integration i ord och handling [Do not say 'meeting place'! Theatre and integration in words and deeds].* Thesis (PhD). Lund University.

4

WAITING

The shrouded backbone of ethnographic research

Pankhuri Agarwal

My fieldwork in Delhi (India) for 7 months in 2019 documented the lived experience of how internal migrant workers[1] in the informal sector navigated the legal system. Even as citizens, internal migrants lose access to welfare rights once they cross the physical boundaries of their home states and move to Delhi because welfare provisions (such as housing and food) are dependent on their proof of residence. The lack of portability of welfare provisions together with the precarious nature of their work such as in sex work, brick kiln work, construction work and others, often leads them to being rescued under the bonded labour and anti-trafficking laws, whether by force, choice or accident.[2] After rescue, they are taken to district courts for determination of their legal status (victim, accused or none), to prisons or shelters depending on their legal status, to courts for trial and to various other state offices for paperwork and rehabilitation assistance. This is a tedious, uncertain and long process that is not linear or time-bound. The aim of my research was to document the post-rescue experience of the workers and its impact on their everyday lives.

The first 3 weeks of the fieldwork were spent waiting in various civil society and government offices, seminars and public events, in an effort to meet people who could introduce me to internal migrant workers. Eventually, I learnt that internal migrant workers may not live in Delhi and may come there only for legal proceedings when ordered by courts or other state institutions from their home states (covering distances as far as 1,300 miles). Even when they lived in Delhi, they usually travelled long distances to these locations. So, there was no option to interview people away from those sites. Expecting them to do so would mean their losing that day's wage, missing transport back to their home state, or even being doubted and scolded by their employer for delays caused by the interview. The only occasion that most of them had any time off from work was when they visited these sites. Therefore, accompanying people to law offices and waiting with them were the only opportunities to do research. For this, I not only needed to know the right place and time to meet people but also to be able to access the sites myself (which required a lot of paperwork for permissions) when workers are there, so as to contextualize their narratives as embedded in these sites with related law enforcement stakeholders.

But this proved difficult in a culture where not being on time is the norm, waiting is normalized and casually filtering information is the *sarkari*[3] way of doing things, as with most bureaucracies around the world. Moreover, relying solely on the observation of interactions between workers and related stakeholders seemed tricky because these interactions usually lasted just a few minutes, preceded and followed by a prolonged wait. I could not follow and document these shorter moments of interaction between the workers and stakeholders over an extended period of time. This is because of institutional and personal constraints around funding, and other issues[4], which did not allow me to conduct research for more than 7 months. At the same time, too, I was unable to schedule anything with the workers outside of these locations, as mentioned above. The only way to do research was therefore to gain permission to enter the law offices and wait with the workers. The fieldwork thus constituted two kinds of waiting: a) waiting outside the research sites to find contacts, network and gain permission to access the sites and b) waiting for and with the workers inside those sites in order to do research. Documenting this waiting or even using it as an analytical and methodological tool was, however, not intended or realized until the end of the fieldwork. In this way, reflecting on the experience of waiting was central to the production of knowledge in this research as all research happened *in waiting* – whether it was waiting to gain access to research sites to engage in participant observation; waiting for legal case files for analysis; or waiting for and with the participants to conduct interviews.

Gradually, a few interlocutors introduced me to different groups of internal migrant workers who were at different stages of legal proceedings. As an oppressed caste[5], internal migrant workers, whether working in Delhi or travelling there because of legal proceedings, endured chronic or prolonged waiting in state and other official sites. Therefore, working with a civil society organization to accompany people to these sites and waiting *with* them afforded me a lot of time to have conversations that ran to several hours' duration. I learnt that their legal cases had lasted between a few months to 37 years.[6] But as I was using this waiting time as an opportunity to do ethnographic research, which would otherwise have been impossible; for the participants, this waiting time was a space of suffering, lost wages (as a result of losing the day's work), increased debt (due to expenses on travel and subsistence to visit legal sites) and of being in limbo for years. Further, our differing social locations did not democratize the experience of being in the law offices or even that of waiting. My middle-class and upper-caste background meant that I had the skills of language and acumen to acquire information to navigate the process of paperwork and legalities. I was also not compelled to wait and could exit these sites whenever I wanted to, while the workers had to continue to wait for the outcome. To conduct fieldwork within these constraints, fieldwork methods included conversational interviewing, participant observation and a study of legal case files.

In this chapter, I begin by discussing the tensions between the constraints of neoliberal time and the debates on what is considered 'real ethnography'. The following

section will draw upon the literature on waiting to demonstrate the scope of waiting for contextualizing participants' narratives in the wider socio-political locations
even before the participants occupy research sites or when the researcher is waiting
to access 'the field'. The third section, based on Bourdieu's (2000) conception of
time and power, will discuss waiting from the perspective of the participants, where
waiting is used to exert control and power over workers' time. I will extend this
conception of waiting by arguing that waiting with the participants offers an opportunity to build relationships based on trust and respect, within time constraints. The
final section will conclude by arguing that even though waiting is an intuitive and
expected state of being in ethnography, actively acknowledging it as a methodological tool in its own right is instrumental to the production of knowledge in the
neoliberal university.

The tension between neoliberal time and the pursuit of 'real ethnography'

> … the secret, beating heart of ethnographic method remains deeply human:
> getting out with a voice recorder, pen and pad, writing, negotiating, hanging
> around, watching, listening, waiting, typing, checking.
>
> (Hamilton 2015, p. 564)

Having roots in anthropology, ethnography presupposes fieldwork and the researcher's immersion in the field from the point of getting access to knowing the field
(Hammersley and Atkinson 2007). Hanging around and waiting in the field is integral to ethnography as ethnography is 'an open-ended, iterative, non-prescriptive
vision for social science, where the researcher is encouraged to acknowledge the
complexity and unpredictability of the research encounter' (Mills and Ratcliffe 2012,
p. 155). However, in contemporary times, there are wide concerns and debates in
doing ethnography in relation to its traditional form – studying a defined spatial site
through participant observation while spending elongated periods of time in the
field. Gupta and Ferguson (1997) argue that the fixed notion of ethnography on
what constitutes 'the field' restricts knowledge production as the meaning of ethnography is expanding with field sites becoming fluid and people being on the move.

Moreover, contemporary academic requirements and constraints around funding, mobility and visa issues[7] do not always allow for spending long periods of time
in the field. This reduction in time in the field comes with its challenges amidst the
requirements of the neoliberal university to be 'academically productive' and to do
more in shorter timeframes (Mountz et al. 2015). Even in the field, researchers are
expected to practise reflexivity without having the time to do so; they are expected
to be effective and credible without always having the time to build relationships
in the field; they are also expected to analyze findings and publish within con-
strained time limits, lest the data be outdated (Hunt 2010). Institutional approaches
to research view research time as buckets to be filled with productive tangible
research activities (Bissell 2007). Thus, what can be done in the field is 'shaped not

simply by intrinsic methodological merits, but by the institutional conditions of intellectual production' (Gupta and Ferguson 1997, p. 23). The increased 'bureaucratization of time' (Jeffrey 2008, p. 954) in the 20th century cannot be felt more than in the requirements of academic research, where, as Moran argues (citing Henry Lefebvre), waiting becomes an 'inevitable product of the bureaucratic appropriation of everyday life' (Moran 2004, p. 219) and hides the exertion of power over people's time by demanding and producing submission. All of this can lead to curtailing the conditions under which traditional ethnography can be done.

Accordingly, what is needed is to decentre the notion of what is conceived as 'the field' from its privileged position in anthropology (which presupposes the resources of time and funding at one's disposal) and to resituate traditional ethnography as one element in a range of methodologies for producing 'situated knowledges' (Haraway 1988). Gupta and Ferguson argue that this transition from a fixed notion of what comprises the field to 'a sense of a mode of study that cares about, and pays attention to, the interlocking of multiple social-political sites and locations' (1997, p. 37) will increase the opportunities for knowledge production where the field cannot be defined by spatial boundaries and people cannot be expected to exist in those spatial boundaries over extended periods of time. This representation of the field is even more necessary when one is researching people on the move, especially in migration and mobility studies.

While the relationship between time and power (Bourdieu 2000) and that of bureaucratic practice has been well studied, waiting has received relatively less scholarly attention (Auyero 2012). Some research has considered waiting as an analytical lens to study waiting as resistance for political mobilization and protest through (in)action (Kracauer 1955, Conlon 2007) as well as active time spent working towards anticipated futures (Axelsson et al. 2015, Brun 2015). Other research discusses waiting as domination to produce exclusion and marginalization by the state's control on people's time (Auyero 2012, Sutton et al. 2015, McNevin and Missbach 2018, Carswell et al. 2019). Even less research exists on looking at waiting from a methodological lens to do useful fieldwork (Mannay and Morgan 2015) or as a period of time where nothing is achieved in the field (Carter 2004, Bissell 2007). However, despite the many usages of waiting to describe the everyday life of people and also their relationship with the everyday state, in disciplines ranging from anthropology, urban studies, sociology and medicine, there exists very little work on the relational experience of waiting in the field as a methodological tool in its own right, and even less in relation to resisting the imperatives of neoliberalism, including that of the neoliberal university. Thus, while waiting is common in ethnographic research, its role is underexplored in writing about the theoretical and methodological aspects of fieldwork.

As discussed in the introduction, the experience of waiting in my fieldwork, just like the field itself, was a series of fragmented threads with untethered stitches where 'the field [...] was not one place that I visited regularly, it was an assembly of places that were continually disrupted, suspended, variously lost and found' (Zengin 2020, p. 346), thus disrupting the traditional notion of ethnography in researching a defined spatial field over extended periods of time. This created the discomfort of questioning whether what I was doing was 'real ethnography'. Accordingly, my initial instinct in field encounters was to fight and negate the experience of waiting, emanating from the fear that, due to long waiting periods, the research might not go anywhere. But, gradually, following people through various sites, making use of waiting time and how people interacted with waiting spaces, along with my own waiting in these spaces, enabled an embodied and relational experience of waiting with the participants (as discussed in the following sections).

Waiting thus provided an alternative, nuanced way to understand people's post-rescue experience with the law by allowing the time to observe the field in ways that went beyond the immediate people or settings needed for research – the body language of people, their interaction with space, the objects they carried, the documents they were asked to produce – all of which gave insights into both the experience of waiting, and the working of the everyday state in India, negotiating which formed a central part of migrants' lives. Further, these observations provided an understanding of the physical characteristics of institutional spaces, of (lack of) accessibility, temporal indeterminacy, and the key aspects of the lived experience of the law. This is more than 'thick description' (Picken 2013, p. 360) (based on the expectation of spending elongated time in the field) as a general orientation in ethnography because this embedded knowledge in waiting required a heightened awareness of space and time. By contextualizing the narratives of the participants in the wider social and political systems, waiting made the pursuit of thick description in ethnographic research merely a means and not an end. However, while waiting, for me, was filled with opportunities to interact with the participants and to contextualize their lived experience with the law, for the participants, waiting was a source of suffering and uncertainty.

Waiting to enter the research sites

This lived experience of 'unjust waiting' was visible in the fieldwork even *before* the participants occupied the research sites. This was when I set out to meet various district, state and central government officials with the hope that they could intro-duce me to field participants and give me permission to enter research sites. These included police officers, district magistrates, ministry and state department officials and labour officers. Finding their contact details, phone numbers and addresses, fix-ing meetings and getting to their offices entailed a lot of waiting time and going around in circles as contact details on their websites were not always updated. Many a time, the buildings had no signposts or directions to rooms. Often, travelling there took a combination of bus, metro, taxi and auto-rickshaw, costing significant money and time, not to mention the drain of energy in Delhi's weather. Despite this, in most cases (barring a few exceptions[8]) there would be hours of waiting as the official concerned would be busy. At other times, it was not because the offices were inaccessible or the official was busy, but because they would not allow access despite my having written permissions from the relevant department controlling access into closed spaces such as women's shelters and prisons. I was made to go around in circles between various state officials for over 2 weeks, and a wait that lasted a month, to get signatures and stamps from various officials. Despite all of this, I was denied entry into some of the spaces.

All of this entailed discomfort that the research might not be going anywhere. However, it was this waiting and going around in circles that gave insights into the working of a bureaucratic system where, despite having networks and knowledge, I could not fit in many meetings at a time. Although this experience of going around in circles, of waiting, of finding the right offices and accessing them, was nothing compared to that of the participants who had been waiting for years, I still experienced how discomforting and debilitating the experience of waiting can be. There could be waiting for an entire day or even weeks. After a while, this waiting time at sites became a source of curiosity into the everyday functioning of state systems, which formed an important part of my research in terms of studying the participants' access to the state and why the laws did not work for them. In hindsight, trying to interview officials who dealt with their cases seemed a near-perfect way of experiencing it first-hand. This pursuit of knowing how waiting impacted the experience of internal migrant workers in accessing the law is palpable in one of my fieldnotes after waiting in a government office that dealt with human rights violations:

> The pass is made. I am sitting in a waiting area, waiting for a senior state official. There are four clerks working under this officer. One is making tea, another is passing files, the third is doing entries on the computer and the fourth is reading a newspaper. The room is so silent that two different clocks can be heard, ticking separately. It is now 1.5 hours I have been waiting. The official has moved from one meeting to another as I can see him walking past the hall. This is understandable. This place deals with urgent cases of human rights violation. It is now 3 hours I have been waiting. The clerk who was reading the newspaper has passed it on to me. He is now drinking tea. He abruptly says, 'All decisions by Sir[9] only.' I respond by asking, 'What decisions?' He replies, 'From buying a chair, meeting people, to giving punishment.' I nod in agreement. There is a poster behind his desk which has a slogan about coming to the office on time. I ask him, 'So, what are your working hours here?' He replies, 'Official time is 9am to 5pm, but we have to stay until Sir leaves.' At this point, Sir comes, looks at me and says, 'Oh, you have come! Give me an hour more.' It is now 3.5 hours I have been waiting.

This experience of waiting gave insights into the functioning of a government office where power is centralized and there is also significant power in the control over the time of subordinate staff. However, while I was sitting in this office next to the official's clerks, other people who had come in respect of their cases had to wait in a central reception area in the building with no means of checking when they would be called. In this way, some waiting areas showed how the spaces for waiting were designed to remind people of their social standing. Who could wait, where and why is indicative of one's social position, purpose of visit and level of knowhow (*jaan-pehchaan*). Waiting in a state office that engaged with everyday cases of informal labour rights violation, I observed that:

> There is a group of buildings in this large compound. Some washrooms can be seen in a row. One of them reads, 'officers' toilet'. After asking people here and there, I have finally found the right building, floor, hallway and room. I have been standing outside an official's room for 5 minutes. A subordinate member of staff comes and says, 'Please wait in the visitors' room.' This room has the dirtiest chairs one could find. One of the walls has a calendar from November 2018. The ceiling has a small fan. There is also a very dirty water filter nearby with plastic cups on the side. There are a few filing cabinets gathering dust. After waiting for 2.5 hours, I get to go inside 'Sir's' office. This is the biggest office I have ever seen. It has more than two air conditioners, good chairs, a huge desk, shining tiles, two computers, clean glasses and more than one 2019 calendar.

This time, I did not get to sit with the staff and instead shared a visitors' room with other people who had come concerning their cases and were frantically sorting their documents should they be called in suddenly; the system appeared to be random, with no queue or numbering system. This difference in spaces (the visitors' area versus the officer's lavish office in the previous excerpt) to designate social inequality can also be seen in classes of train fares, flight tickets and waiting lounges at airports (Gasparini 1995). In this way, space is used as a marker of social difference where a person's social standing is reminded to them. Space, then, can also be a tool to condition people into accepting their place. However, it was not only the stark difference between the waiting areas and the officer's office, but also the treatment that people in these waiting areas were met with. In a state court which dealt with women's protection issues, there was an interesting dimension as to whose waiting was acceptable, where and how:

> After an hour, at 10am, I have finally found the right floor, which is housed in a building with no signposts and looks like a ruin. The waiting area is not separate, but a set of benches lined against a busy, narrow corridor. There is a row of rooms on the other side of this corridor. Each room has a staff member standing outside it with a list of cases to be heard on the day. People come in the morning, show their papers and the staff member ticks their name on the list. It is now 11am and I am waiting. Woman after woman comes in, some alone, others with family or friends. At noon, I ask the person standing

outside 'Ma'am's' room when I will be called. He replies, 'I don't know when Ma'am will come. Everybody is waiting.' It is 1.30pm now. Ma'am is here. Besides me, there are two tribal women dressed in *lehenga choli*[10] with *dupatta*[11] covering their faces. A woman staff member walking in the corridor tells them in a raised, angry voice so everyone can hear, 'Put your feet down and your dupatta up!' The women shift in embarrassment. There is also a very old woman waiting for her turn. She accuses the man standing outside Ma'am's office that he is allowing other people to get in when it is her turn. The man replies angrily, 'It is now lunchtime from 1.30pm to 2pm. The court does not run by your whims!'

Comparing the above three excerpts, the fact that the four clerks in the first excerpt allowed me to sit with them and that the tribal women in the third were a source of annoyance shows how social position determines what stool or bench one can occupy and where. Time and space both get graduated in these encounters, where a person's social standing determines what space they can occupy. Drawing on Foucault, Jeffrey (2010) argues that the state uses its power in very specific ways to condition people to act in certain ways. It can be seen in the state's use of spaces where people must wait, or in its treatment of people in these spaces. The above excerpts show that this power to condition people, to remind them of who they are and where they belong, is also visible in the physical spaces of the state and law institutions. This waiting is not instrumental or technocratic, but is more about hierarchies, by exercising power through people's time while producing a false notion of development, hope and justice because of which people continue to wait.

These observations are a reminder of Franz Kafka's novel *The Trial* (1998). Kafka's universe is a performance of 'absolute and unpredictable power' (Bourdieu 2000, p. 229). In my fieldwork, the iterations that preceded any given meeting with a state official, ranging from making the trip, to finding offices, waiting in the visitors' room, to the actual meeting, are certainly Kafkaesque. Yet, rather than there being the boundary of the gate as in Kafka's universe, such as the issuance of passes in the first excerpt of this section, it is a multilayered reality as though access is carefully graduated, with a stool outside the office, a bench in the hallway, a staff member outside the office. Neither is it the same as the state in Kafka's world where nothing gets done. Something does eventually get done through these graduated, moderated interactions with the state, albeit slowly and incoherently. One file is passed on, one hearing is held, and one signature or stamp is approved, even though each of these seemingly small tasks may take weeks, months or even years. This institutional face of the state is visible in how time is understood, experienced and moderated by those who inhabit it through waiting.

Thus, an observation of the physical design of the waiting areas as well as the embodied relational experience of its inhabitants gave unexpected insights into the social worlds of the research participants *even before they occupied these spaces*. Observation, recording and reflecting as to how people inhabit the waiting spaces, how they arrive and occupy them, the institutional variations in these waiting spaces, and what they understand from it offers the researcher an opportunity to contextualize the social worlds of the participants. This ethnographic experience that is accessible within these waiting times (outside of actual research sites or 'the field') is an underexplored tool in ethnography to contextualize participants' narratives in socio-political locations, especially when there are time constraints in fieldwork.

Waiting with and for the participants *inside* research sites

My fieldnotes have many reflective questions which indicate the central role of waiting in the research: 'How much longer do I wait for the official? Why are people made to come to law offices early in the morning and then made to wait for the whole day as if they have nothing else to do?' As more time was spent with the participants in law offices, they expressed anxiety which accompanied this waiting. They often asked me: 'How long do we wait for? So, do we come tomorrow again? Did you understand what was just discussed or should we wait to ask someone?' Most of the time, I did not know what we were waiting for, for whom and for how long. Even though we often asked these questions (amongst ourselves), we did not feel overly frustrated. After a while, there was a sense of acceptance in waiting. We would comfortably fold our legs on a chair or a bench and have conversations for hours while waiting. Waiting with the research participants and 'waiting upon' (Palmer *et al.* 2018, p. 427) them gave insights into the background conditions of the legal journeys of the people which were not immediately visible.

On some occasions, even when the interviews and observations in research sites were completed, I continued to accompany the participants to those sites and waited with them. I also waited for them when they were sometimes late to arrive for a court hearing. This helped in building trust, a sense of comfort and commitment to the participants as well as the research. One day, I was waiting outside a district magistrates' court for Abeera[12], an oppressed-class Muslim domestic worker in Delhi. It was the day when, finally, she would be 'heard' in the case of non-payment of minimum wages and physical violence at work. She was a few minutes late as she had to complete cleaning people's houses before coming to the court. She came running in. I told her to relax and that we would probably have to wait anyway. She sat down, caught her breath and said, 'I am always the one waiting from morning to evening in courts. Nobody has waited for me before.' Even though the power relations between the researcher and the participants are an undeniable presence in the field, the shared moments of waiting provide the opportunity to respect the 'others' time and to address power imbalances, by postponing research needs to make space for the needs of the participants.

As I continued to wait with Abeera in various law offices, we did not always talk. We shared glances, sighed in frustration while enduring indefinite waiting, and offered water and food to each other. But I still learnt a lot about the background conditions of her everyday life which were affected because of the legal proceedings. She spent money on travelling to each of these sites, not to mention the significant physical and mental impact on her body for over 3 years. While waiting, she would constantly call and check on her three children – had they eaten food? Had they taken their medicine? She also went outside many times to meet her husband, who was a rickshaw driver and would come to see her to take updates whenever he did not have a passenger. She also evolved through the months as she gathered information, made contacts and tried to figure out ways to please or navigate the state bureaucracy by becoming a disciplined worker who could wait for hours. Thus, in waiting spaces, a lot happened – checking on family, arranging food, asking questions, sorting paperwork, gaining knowledge, etc. This suggests that, for those waiting, life goes on through the experience of elongated times (Povinelli 2011).

With Abeera, courts also became a site of unique revelation where it was normalized to see a poor person's time and their existence as disposable and unimportant. The court hierarchy had different kinds of waiting areas. High courts had waiting rooms, whereas at district courts one had to wait in corridors. The numbering system in high courts was on a digital board, while in district courts it was printed on a sheet of A4 paper outside the courtroom. The numbering system was a super-confusing one that only lawyers and people in the system could understand. The list was released a night before unless someone was coming from outside Delhi, in which case they were notified further in advance. People came to the court in the morning and waited till evening. The lawyers would know when their clients would be called, and they arrived accordingly near the time. Since the workers lived far away, the lawyers preferred that they came in the morning and waited, rather than risk their clients being late. Many a time, workers were not required at all hearings. However, their destitute appearance[13] suggested the urgency of the case itself. Sometimes, even after waiting for the whole day, they would not be called because either the day was over, or one of the counsels was not present, or simply for other reasons. The workers would go home, again incurring travel expenses. On one of the days, waiting in a district court with three oppressed-caste women who had journeyed for three days over 1,300 miles from Assam to be present for a court hearing in Delhi, my fieldnotes read:

> I come with them to the court at 9am. We sit outside the judge's office on a bench in a hallway. There is a small fan diagonally placed on the wall outside this office. The clerk keeps switching it on and off. One of the women has a 5-month-old baby boy in her lap. When the fan is off, the child cries and she takes the child to another hallway where a fan is on. It has now been 3 hours and we are still waiting. After 3 hours, when we are called inside, the judge's chamber has an air conditioner and looks newly built, unlike the hallway we were sitting in with gloomy walls, paint peeling off them. The lawyers are told that no statement will be taken today because the public prosecutor is on election duty or something. He will come after a week and then we must come again for the statement. The women worry about their old parents in a village in Assam. The court also does not reimburse their food receipts nor give them a place to live for this week when they must wait for the next hearing.

The above excerpt illustrates how much is happening in the waiting time. Most officials do not function on time, yet it is the oppressed who is expected to arrive early and wait in anticipation with hope and documents. People are kept in the dark regarding the length of waiting time and what paperwork is required. So, when a person meets the state through a window counter or in an office, they are told that someone is not present, or some paperwork is missing. They are told to come back some other day. Not knowing what to expect is part of the strategy of domination, where 'interactions with the state have their one-way streets, their no-entry signs, their things to say and not say and things to do and to avoid doing, their obligations and penalties' (Bourdieu 2000, p. 161).

But this waiting happens not only inside law offices, but also outside them. People who travelled from other cities or states to take part in legal proceedings usually spent time living in night shelters in deplorable conditions and did not have the money for food and other necessities. The woman in the above excerpt shared in the court hearing a week later: 'The shelter is dirty. Drug addicts live there. When we go out to the court, they talk behind our back that we must be doing some shady work.' She had taken out a loan for food and travel to Delhi. She was constantly thinking about many problems at once as a result of this extended period of waiting for the hearing: the worry of repaying the debt, along with taking care of her child and old parents in Assam constantly distressed her. This experience of delayed time is also experienced as that of 'otherness and failure' as it 'occurs when people are required to live up to the hegemonic temporalities that are set by others, but [are] not provided with the means to do so' (Kjærre 2018, p. 3). In a way, by making people wait for the entire day only to be told to come later, it provides 'a critical insight into the everyday socio-spatial constitution of power – not despite but because of their banality' (Secor 2007, p. 42, cited in Auyero 2012). Therefore, an exploration of the relational knowledge of waiting inside and outside the research sites challenges and expands the boundaries of what is considered a research site or the field in ethnography.

Waiting at law offices shows not only the state's power which dominated people's time and made it difficult for them to access justice at every step of the way but also how the system was broken from within: sometimes, *even the state did not know how to access itself.* Though each government office has a theoretical organizational structure (usually displayed on a board outside), its working on the ground is rather muddled. In some ways, the state is unknowable from both the outside and inside. One day, I was waiting in a police station with Malin, a Dalit informal worker from Uttarakhand, so that he could be taken to the magistrates' court to record his statement against non-payment of wages and physical violence in Delhi. My fieldnotes from the day read:

> Malin and I have travelled for 2 hours and have been waiting in this police station from 10am. Waiting here is not a very comforting experience. There are dark, dingy, smelly locker-rooms. Police personnel are running from here to there attending to something. We are sitting on a bench. A well-off man

dressed in branded clothes and shoes with sunglasses walks in with confidence as if this is his own house. The police attend to this well-off man immediately and he walks out of the station in no time. It is now 2.5 hours that we have been waiting. A police inspector has now ordered his subordinate to bring a car out so we can go to the district court. The subordinate gets worried and is trying to find where the court is. It is 1pm now and they bring a car and tell us to sit in it. We enter the court and it is like the busiest railway platform. The court's staff are working peacefully amidst this chaos as if they are in a meditation centre. The police personnel are trying to find the magistrates' court. They find the room, but it is empty. A man (clerk to the judge) comes from behind and tells the police, 'Sir is having lunch. Wait outside.' There are not enough chairs to wait on. So, I ask Malin to sit since he looks dehydrated and sick. After an hour, we ask the clerk, 'When will Sir come?' He responds casually, 'Can't say. He is now in a meeting. It can take half an hour, or even one hour.' Malin is worried that if he spends too much time here, his employer might fire him from the job. After an hour, Sir comes, and a stream of people follow him. We stand there looking *up* at him, as he sits on a huge chair behind a magnificent table on a heightened cement platform in the room. And then half an hour later, our turn comes, finally!

The case was not completed despite this waiting, but that is a discussion for elsewhere. Bourdieu's (2000) work shows the role of time in people's everyday life and how it determines how people navigate power relations. He shows the difference in how privileged classes manage to enter, navigate and get through complex spaces and fields. However, the poor, being in a subordinated position, lack the resources, networks and knowledge as they lack 'the spatio-temporal acuity that comes with routine success' (Jeffrey 2010, p. 20). So, workers in my research knew, and had become habituated to, waiting, not being heard or answered, being neglected, ignored or taken for granted. They entered these sites knowing they would wait. In such research encounters, the researcher's role in the waiting field becomes even more important. Waiting for the participants, taking into account their time and delays, as well as waiting with them, the ethnographer can also lend support, and embrace the uncertainty and long waiting times by prioritizing people's needs before their own research requirements. As Palmer *et al.* assert, 'The researcher's waiting is thus always relational: they wait upon another's needs and priorities in a way that supports the other to participate, as they also wait for the other to make their contribution so that the project can proceed' (2018, p. 428).

This acceptance of the other's time is an integral part of ethnographic encounters. In the fieldwork, as a fieldworker who was accompanying people through these various law offices, I was responsible for writing formal letters and getting them stamped by officials on the participants' behalf. These acts happened in the waiting field, when the participants usually either looked over my shoulder or sat silently. These were also times when we shared our collective anger, anxieties, worries and modes of navigating the legal process, although in different contexts (they were part of the legal process and I was merely an outsider to it). In this way, waiting provided an opportunity for not only the building of trusting and respectful relationships and to address the power relations, but also moments of shared time and recognition in the field that is otherwise all about domination and inequality. It enabled the shaping of questions and issues together with the participants by making the experience of waiting a tool for explaining the concept of state domination in my research.

Conclusion

This chapter has shown that the practice of waiting, even though expected and intuitive in ethnography, is underemployed in writing on methodology. I have argued for the role of waiting as a fieldwork tool in its own right to sustain a methodological commitment to ethnography in the presence of institutional and other constraints. The quote from Hamilton's work that started the section on the tension between neoliberal time and ethnography illustrates how 'hanging out' and 'waiting' is part of ethnography (Hamilton 2015). I would like to contend that this hanging out and waiting is also crucial outside of the research sites, as illustrated in the section on that aspect. As shown, for the researcher, waiting time is active time spent on collecting the empirics (waiting itself as a source of knowledge) when scheduling meetings with participants in defined space or time is impossible. It helps the researcher to contextualize participants' narratives in the wider social and political systems in ways which might otherwise be impossible when faced with time constraints. From the standpoint of the participants, waiting shows a difference in social standing even when people are not occupying the research sites. When people occupy these spaces, it shows the role of power relations, marginalization and domination over their time to exclude them even as citizens.

A meta-reflection in writing this chapter has been about the limits of writing on waiting. The waiting time as shared between the participants and myself is certainly not equal in fieldwork. The experience and representation of this experience are also indicative of that inequality. In fact, the writing of this chapter feeds into neoliberal academia by producing something that will hopefully benefit my academic career. Ethical dilemmas surround the benefit which I have been able to draw from this experience, while the participants continue to wait. Thus, reflecting on waiting and writing about it from the standpoint of the researcher and the participants – what is gained and lost; what is active and passive; what comprises the field and what does not – are all constitutive of the ethnographic experience and raise ethical discomfort.

This chapter also invites a more general engagement with waiting as an opportunity for building trusting relationships, contextualizing the past, present and future narratives of the participants as well as to practise relational reflexivity – all of which are core components of ethnographic research. The universe of waiting described in this chapter during fieldwork could easily be the state in various situations of the social world of oppressed, stigmatized groups and will be interesting to those doing ethnographic research at multiple sites where the field cannot be marked spatially, where there is no control of time, where the researcher must submit to the clock of these sites and the routines of its people, thus incurring waiting such as in hospitals and factories. It will also be useful to those in migration and mobility studies to contextualize their methodological dilemmas and discomforts while constantly moving with the participants in limited timeframes and with institutional and other limits.

In the midst of a world pandemic, with further deliberations about new thinking on ethnography, waiting as a methodological tool is a useful way to think about what constitutes the ethnographic field: many are in a country of fieldwork but not in the field; the connotations of entering the field, being in the field, and leaving it are also evolving with the changing meanings of seeing the field as more than a physical boundary; the experience of time globally vis-à-vis the neoliberal university is being felt differently. In other words, waiting is becoming a more relational, transitory and embodied experience at the centre of understanding and respecting the past, present and future locations and experiences of researchers, the research and the participants. It is no longer the time between events or actions; it is at the centre of all events and actions in the field. It disrupts, expands, discomforts and redefines an ethnographer's vision of the field through complete submission to the clock of 'the field'[14].

Notes

1 Internal migrant workers move for work or other reasons within India. For context, see Abbas (2016), Deshingkar (2017) and others.

2 The laws that address bonded labour (The Bonded Labour System (Abolition) Act 1976) and human trafficking (Immoral Traffic (Prevention) Act 1956) in India presume a rescue and rehabilitation approach. 'Rescue' means the legal removal of a person from a work situation that is perceived as forced and exploitative under the above two laws. For context, see Shah (2014), Ramachandran (2015), Kimberley (2016) and others.

3 Meaning the state's accepted way of working. This is indicative of the tacit knowledge of the state's functioning as embedded in the wider bureaucratic culture which no one talks about explicitly, but everyone is expected to know. For example, when one enters a government office, it is with the assumption that one must wait because there will be delays. This would be one of the '*sarkari*' ways of knowing or doing things. On the state's functioning in India and other bureaucracies around the world, see Scott (1998), Gupta (2012), Mathur (2016) and others.

4 I am grateful to the Socio-Legal Studies Association for supporting me with a fieldwork grant, which allowed me to spend 7 months in the field. Besides funding and visa issues, gendered and personal constraints around how much time one can spend away from 'home' also determine the time in the field.

5 Workers who are from the oppressed caste such as Dalits. On caste and the caste system in India, see Vishwanath (2014), Guru and Sarukkai (2019) and others.

6 Research participants are at different stages of the legal process, awaiting completion of rehabilitation assistance for as long as 37 years. During these years, because of the promise of state rehabilitation, workers keep waiting while continuing with their life, engaging in similar or more exploitative work than that from which they were first rescued. For some other workers, such as those engaged in sex work, they wait for the trial to end so that they do not have to appear at court hearings and can continue with their work.

7 Even if a researcher is doing fieldwork in a country in which they are a citizen (like India in my case), long-term fieldwork with adequate university permissions and ethical clearances is equated with 'excess absence' and can be used against the researcher in future visa applications in the country of study (in this context, the UK). Many international academics have been subjected to this hostile and ambivalent interpretation of visa regulations in the UK. See Dowson (2018), Scialom (2020) and others.

8 Some state officials, lawyers, social workers and comrades (who remain anonymous here) were very receptive towards my research. They helped me to contextualize the field in the past and present socio-political locations, enabled access to research sites and introduced me to the field participants. I remain grateful to them for their engagement and inspiration.

9 'Sir' and 'Ma'am' are used to address or refer to those in authority, for example, teachers, professors, government officials and colleagues in higher positions.

10 A traditional Indian attire comprising a long skirt and a blouse.

11 A long piece of cloth used with traditional clothing to cover the front of the body and the head.

12 All the field participants' names have been replaced by pseudonyms to protect their identities. I would like to express my gratitude and indebtedness to them for their time, trust and generosity in sharing their stories and for their ongoing involvement in the research.

13 Many a time, some social workers explicitly asked the workers to take off their jewellery or to not arrive in good clothes. On the other hand, for some workers, these visits to law offices were the only times they could 'go out' and so they wanted to dress properly, even with limited means.

14 Besides the co-authors and workshop mentors involved in this volume, I would like to express my appreciation to the following friends and colleagues for their labour and time in critically reading various parts and drafts of this chapter: Angelo Martins Junior, Joel Quirk, Judith Onwubiko, Julia O'Connell Davidson, Katie Cruz, Maayan Niezna and Simanti Dasgupta. Their feedback helped me to question my biases and assumptions in critical methodological writing.

References

Abbas, R., 2016. Internal migration and citizenship in India. *Journal of Ethnic and Migration Studies*, 42 (1), 150–168.

Auyero, J., 2012. *Patients of the state*. Durham; London: Duke University Press.

Axelsson, L., Malmberg, B. and Zhang, Q., 2015. On waiting, work-time and imagined futures: Theorising temporal precariousness among Chinese chefs in Sweden's restaurants industry. *Geoforum*, 78, 169–178.

Bissell, D., 2007. Animating suspension: Waiting for mobilities. *Mobilities*, 2 (2), 277–298.

Bourdieu, P., 2000. *Pascalian meditations*. Palo Alto, CA: Stanford University Press.

Brun, C., 2015. Active waiting and changing hopes: Toward a time perspective on protracted displacement. *Social Analysis*, 59 (1), 19–37.

Carswell, G., Chambers, T. and De Neve, G., 2019. Waiting for the state: Gender, citizenship and everyday encounters with bureaucracy in India. *EPC: Politics and Space*, 37 (4), 597–616.

Carter, P., 2004. *Material thinking: The theory and practice of creative research*. Melbourne: Melbourne University Press.

Conlon, D., 2007. *The nation as embodied practice: Women, migration and the social production of nationhood in Ireland*. Thesis (PhD). City University of New York.

Deshingkar, P., 2017. Towards contextualised, disaggregated and intersectional understandings of migration in India. *Asian Population Studies*, 13 (2), 119–123.

Dowson, N., 2018. Durham University academics given two weeks to leave UK [online]. *The Guardian*. Available from: https://www.theguardian.com/uk-news/2018/mar/16/durham-university-academics-given-two-weeks-leave-uk-home-office-ruling-legal-challenge [Accessed 12 October 2020].

Gasparini, G., 1995. On waiting. *Time and Society*, 4 (1), 29–45.

Gupta, A., 2012. *Red Tape: Bureaucracy, structural violence, and poverty in India*. Durham and London: Duke University Press.

Gupta, A. and Ferguson, J., 1997. Discipline and practice: 'The field' as site, method, and location in anthropology'. In: A. Gupta and J. Ferguson, eds. *Anthropological locations: Boundaries and grounds of field science*. Berkeley, Los Angeles and London: University of California Press, 101–146.

Guru, G. and Sarukkai, S., 2019. *Experience, caste, and the everyday social*. New Delhi, India: Oxford University Press.

Hamilton, L., 2015. When I ask myself these questions. *Ethnography*, 16 (4), 556–565.

Hammersley, M. and Atkinson, P., 2007. *Ethnography: Principles in practice*. New York: Routledge.

Haraway, D., 1988. Situated knowledges: The science question in feminism and the privilege of partial perspective. *Feminist Studies*, 14 (3), 575–599.

Hunt, M.R., 2010. 'Active waiting': Habits and the practice of conducting qualitative research. *International Journal of Qualitative Methods*, 9 (1), 69–76.

Jeffrey, C., 2008. Waiting. *Environment and Planning D: Society and Space*, 26, 954–958.

Jeffrey, C., 2010. *Timepass: Youth, class, and the politics of waiting in India*. Stanford, CA: Stanford University Press.

Kafka, F., 1998. *The Trial*. New York: Schochen Books.

Kimberley, W., 2016. Humanitarian trafficking: Violence of rescue and (mis)calculation of rehabilitation. *Economic and Political Weekly*, 44–45, 55–61.

Kjærre, H.A., 2018. *Waiting around? On temporal irregularity and im/mobility among Afghans within Europe* [online]. *WAIT Project*, University of Bergen. Available from: https://www.uib.no/en/project/wait/121783/waiting-around-temporal-irregularity-and-immobility-among-afghans-within-europe [Accessed 25 September 2020].

Kracauer, S., 1955. *The Mass Ornament*. Cambridge, MA: Harvard University Press.

Mannay, D. and Morgan, M., 2015. Doing ethnography or applying a qualitative technique? Reflections from the waiting field. *Qualitative Research*, 15 (2), 166–182.

Mathur, N., 2016. *Paper Tiger: Law, bureaucracy, and the developmental state in Himalayan India*. Delhi: Cambridge University Press.

McNevin, A. and Missbach, A., 2018. Luxury limbo: Temporal techniques of border control and the humanitarianisation of waiting. *International Journal of Migration and Border Studies*, 4 (1–2), 12–34.

Mills, D. and Ratcliffe, R., 2012. After method? Ethnography in the knowledge economy. *Qualitative Research*, 15 (2), 166–182.

Moran, J., 2004. November in Berlin: The end of the everyday. *History Workshop Journal*, 57, 216–234.

Mountz, A. et al., 2015. For slow scholarship: A feminist politics of resistance through collective action in the neoliberal university. *ACME: An International E-Journal for Critical Geographies*, 14 (4), 1235–1259.

Palmer, J., Pacock, C. and Burton, L., 2018. Waiting, power and time in ethnographic and community-based research. *Qualitative Research*, 18 (4), 416–432.

Picken, F., 2013. Ethnography. In: M. Walter, ed. *Social research methods*. 3rd ed. Melbourne: Oxford University Press, 337–350.

Povinelli E.A., 2011. *Economies of Abandonment: Social belonging and endurance in late liberalism*. Durham: Duke University Press.

Ramachandran, V., 2015. Rescued but not released: The 'protective custody' of sex workers in India [online]. *Open Democracy*. Available from: https://www.opendemocracy.net/en/beyond-trafficking-and-slavery/rescued-but-not-released-protective-custody-of-sex-workers-in-i/ [Accessed 10 October 2020].

Scialom, M., 2020. Home Office's 'strategic incompetence' is to reduce immigration, says Dr Asiya Islam [online]. *Cambridge Independent*. Available from: https://www.cambridgeindependent.co.uk/news/home-office-s-strategic-incompetence-is-to-reduce-immigration-says-dr-asiya-islam-9101262/ [Accessed 12 October 2020].

Scott, J.C., 1998. *Seeing Like a State: How certain schemes to improve the human condition have failed*. New Haven, NJ: Yale University Press.

Secor, A., 2007. Between longing and despair: State, space and subjectivity in Turkey. *Environment and Planning D: Society and Space*, 25, 33–52.

Shah, S., 2014. *Street Corner Secrets: Sex, work, and migration in the city of Mumbai*. Durham: Duke University Press.

Sutton, R., Vigneswaran, D. and Wels, H., 2015. Waiting in liminal space: Migrants' queuing for Home Affairs in South Africa. *Anthropology Southern Africa*, 34 (1–2), 30–37.

Vishwanath, R., 2014. *The Pariah Problem: Caste, religion, and the social in modern India*. New York: Columbia University Press.

Zengin, A., 2020. A field of silence: Secrecy, intimacy, and sex work in Turkey. *Feminist Studies*, 46 (2), 345–370.

5

MIDDLE-CLASSNESS

Research object and fieldwork performance

Katrine Scott

In 2012 (February, and October–December), I engaged in fieldwork with university students in Sulaimani, Iraqi Kurdistan. It was a relatively peaceful moment in the city situated in a region affected by ongoing war and conflict. The findings in my dissertation show that narratives of apolitical middle-class aspirations were central in students' accounts of a liveable future beyond political conflict and war (Scott 2018).

I participated in lectures, conversations and recorded interviews with students at both the private American University of Iraq, Sulaimani (AUIS) and the public University of Sulaimani (UOS). AUIS was established in 2007, to provide a liberal arts education in English, four years after the US-led invasion in which Denmark took part. UOS was free of charge, and education was in Sorani Kurdish, Arabic and English. I talked with students mainly in English, and for a few interviews there was an interpreter present to help translate between Sorani Kurdish and English. I had learned to navigate, with basic language skills, in Sorani Kurdish. With my mobility privilege from holding a Danish passport, I had stayed in Sulaimani several times between 2008 and 2012. I was visiting Sulaimani not only as a researcher, but also as a family member since my partner at the time had grown up in the region. Prior to the fieldwork in 2012, I had also been part of organizing a workshop on youth activism together with both Kurdish and Danish youth, and I had been engaged in carrying out interviews for my BA thesis in gender studies with different activists and organizations in Sulaimani working with gender perspectives and women's rights.

Middle-classness in different places

'If they are just like us, why should we read about them?' This question was posed to me at a research seminar in Scandinavia, while discussing my unfinished work with university students in Iraqi Kurdistan and their middle-class aspirations. The question pointed out a central tension in my study about middle-class commonalities and differences across geographies: a tension that I was trying to grapple with and understand, and might not, in the draft prepared for the seminar, have succeeded very well in unfolding. The question also indicated that an audience in the Global North expects to read in research about lives that are 'different' in the Global South. I do not recall exactly what my response was at that moment, but the fact that I remember the question so clearly is connected to my indignation at the possibility of asking this question as if it were the most obvious thing in the world. The fact that it was possible to ask this question could be understood as a general uninterest in ordinary everyday life outside of Scandinavia. This type of question, or uninterest that I had also experienced at other times, spurred my already-existing determinedness to highlight commonalities in global patterns of middle-classness in my study as a response to what I perceived to be a desire for difference that I felt uncomfortable. This determinedness was also related to my initial motivation for the research project that grew out of the context of Denmark, where I resided, being part of the US-led invasion in Iraq in 2003, and the lack of nuanced media representations of the region in Denmark. Ordinary, urban middle-class everyday life was not part of the media coverage on war and conflict, and the effect was to create representations of populations in war-torn regions as ontologically 'different' from the middle class in Europe consuming these news stories. With my research, I wanted to challenge that representation. I heard the question at the seminar as an academic version of the media's interest in war only.

One aspect that could be read from the 'If they are just like us, why should we read about them?' question is ideas of 'appropriate' research subjects for critical feminist research. Esther Priyadharshini studied privileged university students in elite MBA programmes in India, and she describes how she was likewise asked: 'Why do we need to study these people?' (Priyadharshini 2003, p. 424). Risa Whitson was asked why she had decided to do research with privileged women working as direct sales consultants instead of 'meaningful' research with less privileged groups of people. This question led her to ask herself: 'Have I chosen the wrong group to work with?

Maybe direct sales consultants are not an appropriate subject for critical feminist research' (Whitson 2017, p. 302). In the 'If they are just like us, why should we read about them?' question regarding my project, I found it analogous to the questioning of the importance of studying relative privilege.

Another aspect to the question is that it shows Eurocentrism at its finest when expressing interest in all that is pointed out as 'different' from one's own position so that one's position stays stable and unquestioned. The question bubbling to the surface in the setting of the academic space for collective thinking shows an underlying desire for the 'exotic' in the seminar room and thereby placing the 'ordinary' in the Global North – a desire for consumption of difference or, to use bell hooks' phrase, 'eating the Other' (hooks 2015[1992], p. 21). This desire and consumption was 'no news' at a time when the figure of the heroic Kurdish female fighter became a poster girl in Western media representations (Dirik 2014). To meet a version of this expectation and desire for 'difference' in the seminar room told me just how rooted and normalized a colonial gaze and construction of the 'Other' is also in research settings presenting themselves as critical. Research is never only an individual project; texts are shaped also by academic discussions. The question, and other similar questions, or simply uninterest, for the project I have met along the way did not open up for an important discussion of commonalities and differences between middle-class trajectories in the Global South and North. What I perceived as uninterest stood in the way of the possibility to collectively develop critical and complex academic thought that questions colonial structures in the knowledge production in which I was embedded.

As a PhD student located in Sweden and Denmark and doing research with students in Iraqi Kurdistan, there is a concrete geographical distance between the context of the students' lived experiences and the official academic place of validating the written analysis. This distance played into the discussions of my work on middle-classness, and questions about commonalities and differences have followed me during my research process. I recently told a new colleague about what the research project showed in relation to the university students' middle-class aspirations, and I was surprisingly met with the comment that the colleague had engaged in a similar project with young people in Denmark about their future aspirations. This was a cross-geographical comparison between Scandinavia and Iraqi Kurdistan that I have rarely come across.

In this chapter, I will revisit my fieldwork and written analysis from a distance of several years later. Imagining the research project as a patchwork of different pieces of material, I will zoom in and look at the stitches that held together my methodological and analytical approach in the study. I argue that my attempt to highlight commonalities in global middle-classness created both opportunities but also obstacles. I will give examples of where my ethnographic approach sometimes limited me, and where it at other times enabled understanding. Today, I look at the study that I conducted as an attempt to 'study sideways' (Nader 1972) between myself as a PhD student with middle-class background and aspirations, and university students in Iraqi Kurdistan with middle-class background and/or aspirations. I did not use the concept of 'sideways' at the time of my fieldwork or in my analysis, but I am using it here as a productive tool to reflect on both methodological and analytical questions and pitfalls related to representations of commonalities and differences in my study with university students. I suggest thinking about 'sideways' across geographical contexts as complex, shifting and embedded in unequal power relations. I reflect on how this attempt to meet students sideways does not step outside of the uneven distribution of mobility privilege and the colonial legacy of being able to do 'international' research in Iraqi Kurdistan and constitute myself as the knowing subject as a scholar from Scandinavia. I argue for a critical reflection of what are perceived as commonalities in research, and when these are considered interesting, and at the same time I also want to broaden the concept of 'sideways' and the perception of when and where it is possible to study commonalities.

The chapter is structured as follows: First, I discuss the concept of 'sideways' together with the methodological concept of 'matching strategies' (Gunaratnam 2003). Through the concepts of sideways and matching, I revisit reflections on what it entails to study middle-classness among university students while at the same time embodying a middle-class position as a researcher from a university in Sweden. I explore the tension between middle-classness both as a research object and what I call a *fieldwork performance* by the researcher. I discuss how fieldwork performances can both enable and set up limits to knowing. I consider a central moment of discomfort in writing about, analyzing and participating in performances of gendered and heterosexual middle-class respectability (Skeggs 1997) that keep up appearances and risk reifying unspoken differences by assuming a common gendered respectability. Finally, I discuss fieldwork performances as taking place both in the field and as representations in the written analysis.

Directions: Studying sideways and matching strategies

In a famous text on methodology, Laura Nader (1972) writes about 'studying up' in one's own society, stating that anthropology in the US in the 1960s was preoccupied with marginalized people's experiences, described as 'studying down', and less on studying the upper or middle classes. Nader writes about the directions of studying up versus down that '[w]e are not dealing with an either/or proposition; we need simply to realize when it is useful or crucial to study up, down or sideways' (Nader 1972, p. 292). My study with university students from middle-class background or with middle-class aspirations while I was a graduate student and had a middle-class background myself can be described by Nader's term of 'studying sideways' (also see Bowman 2009 and Plesner 2011), which I will expound, question and develop in this chapter since positions in hierarchies are not that simple. I am using the concept of studying sideways here to reflect on directions in research and questions of commonalities and difference.

Studying other students while being a student oneself is described by Laura E. Hirshfield, who studied graduate students in chemistry while she was herself a graduate student, as studying sideways when studying her 'peers' who were people 'like her' (Hirshfield and Ramahi 2018, p. 2). Hirshfield, as a graduate student in the field of social science, was both a 'naïve observer' in the field of chemistry and at the same time a 'native graduate student' (Hirshfield and Ramahi 2018, p. 6). She describes how she and her research participants met in a shared position as graduate students in the power hierarchy of the university, but also how that shared position contained assumptions about shared similarities that were unfounded. On the other hand, Hirshfield notes that the graduate students in her study 'did not feel judged' by her (Hirshfield and Ramahi 2018, p. 8). Studying sideways among her presumed 'peers' gave Hirshfield opportunities in terms of sharing equal positions in the university setting, but it also created assumptions about sameness. Hirshfield's reflection on the taken-for-granted and therefore unexplored assumptions about sameness among students is a central concern in studying sideways since the direction of sideways builds on the idea of similarity. My study with university students as a graduate student myself also contained questions around shared and different experiences and positions. Like Hirshfield, to a great extent, I also experienced a connection with (some, not all) students as another young adult and as some kind of student who was not their teacher in a higher position in the university hierarchy.

While the concept of studying sideways provides an image of a horizontal line and the idea of standing side by side as researcher and researched, 'matching strategies' is another term used in qualitative methods looking more into the content of supposed matching through similarities between researcher and researched. 'Matching strategies' are sometimes used in qualitative interview studies with the aim of better communication if interviewer and interviewee share some perceived commonalities such as gender and ethnicity/'race' (Gunaratnam 2003). The focus is on the strategic choice of trying to find a match between researcher and researched, whereas the concept of studying sideways indicates a somewhat fixed analysis of positions in hierarchies and power relations. The idea of matching as a deliberate methodological strategy demands reflection around those perceived shared experiences and positions. Yasmin Gunaratnam discusses the complex idea of 'racial matching' (Gunaratnam 2003, p. 103), that risks not only presupposing shared commonalities based on 'race' but also not seeing differences despite 'racial matching', such as, for example, class. But on the other hand, 'racial matching' in research on racism – not as a solution but as one strategy – might have the potential to open for conversations about racialized experiences. The tension lies in how to take into account the lived experiences and materiality of a racialized world while at the same time questioning the category of 'race' in fieldwork and analysis (Gunaratnam 2003). The concept of matching also brings into focus the fact that matches and mismatches will always affect the study regardless of the researcher's awareness. Looking back at my own research, I somehow tried to 'middle-class match' as a research strategy. While 'racial matching strategies' might have the aim of creating spaces to talk about lived experiences of racism and of being dominated, middle-class matching points to a very different kind of shared experience of privilege and dominance. What I was trying to 'match' was an experience of relative privilege in terms of class position and aspiration, thereby situating myself as a PhD student side by side with university students in Sulaimani in what I presumed to be somewhat middle-class matching positions, with the risk of not being attentive enough to mismatching and differences (also see Lacy 2019 on strategies for studying black middle classes in US suburbs). Based on my experience, I suggest thinking about the concepts of sideways and matching as fluid and unstable. I argue for not limiting the idea of studying sideways to a very narrow understanding of what and where a shared context can take place. I also argue that the direction of 'sideways' needs to be thoroughly examined as to how power relations shape the research process and fieldwork.

Unseen areas when studying sideways and trying to match

My research centred on exploring young, well-educated people's everyday lives and dreams in the big city scene, to capture and investigate what I saw as relative, fragile privilege in a region affected by war. My drive inspiring this exploration was to study aspects of life that I imagined, and had previous experiences of, would in some ways relate to and reflect patterns of global middle-class life in many big cities – a life in some ways resembling the one that I also lived myself. Looking back, this could be seen as a fixed category of class transcending social context and sidestepping a more specific focus on differences in the relationship between researcher and researched. In my methodological approach, that I label as an attempt to study 'sideways' and to 'middle-class match', I was determined to see myself to some extent as standing alongside students due to my initial motivation to study their unspectacular everyday lives and dreams in the city. I did not assume similarities in the same way as Hirshfield did in her study with graduate students in chemistry, but I placed experiences on a horizontal line side by side, categorizing them as the same – placing students' middle-class dreams of a future beside the dreams of students globally.

An important aspect that could be overlooked when viewing from a horizontal perspective is different possibilities in mobility. I experienced a couple of students who asked how to apply for scholarships to study at a Swedish university. They might have participated in interviews with me in the hope of getting information and help to go abroad and study. I provided information and showed students where they could read more about opportunities to study in Sweden, but I went no further in assisting students with this. Nobody asked for my more specific help – maybe because I did not volunteer it. I could have practised providing more information and assistance in an organized way such as some scholars do in critical migration studies, but I was not prepared (see Düvell et al. 2009). A central question is to ask how Global North–South relations were present and 'disturbing' or 'haunting' the fieldwork and analysis (also see Gunaratnam on how structural whiteness can 'haunt' and 'disturb' an analysis (Gunaratnam 2003, p. 92). The example of asking for information about scholarships shows how Global North–South relations were present and affecting my meetings with students. I was in a position of power to provide them with knowledge about admission to a system of education that could potentially provide them with a degree from abroad that could transform into a good job in Iraqi Kurdistan. The value of degrees from a European university was ambivalent for me since I held a privileged position in a Eurocentric ranking system of higher education that I did not politically approve of. I was confronted with my own unspoken hope to meet indifference to this ranking among students and pride in local higher education, a hope from a secure position with my privilege of being able to travel and do research at a university abroad that also added value to my doctoral education. The uneven distribution of mobility privilege positioned me and my research participants differently, and this inequality was a backdrop to our everyday encounters. The immersion into the everyday life I was trying to navigate put practical matters at the forefront, such as arranging meetings with students, building relationships and thinking about whether people wanted to meet and talk with me or not. The inequality in mobility was often just a distant jarring sound on top of which everything else happened. Now, several years later when the experience has turned into text, it is much easier to reflect clearly on the unequal distribution of possibilities of movement and access to what counts as highly ranked universities and how that plays differently into the possible horizon for future aspirations.

Matching gendered respectability

As a specific example of studying sideways and trying to match, I experienced an ongoing occupation of dealing with boundaries in performing the right kind of respectability, especially in my encounters with female students. Matching is not only a strategy that can be methodologically thought about beforehand, but it is also a fieldwork performance that we can engage in as researchers. My notion of fieldwork performance is inspired by Butler's concept of performativity (Butler 1990) since I want to capture the contextual *doings* of researcher and researched in fieldwork. An example of this is a conversation I had with Sehla and Avin, two female students from AUIS. In my thesis, I write about the experience of waiting and highlight a conversation where we talk about time and making family plans. During the conversation, I say that I am not in Sulaimani on my own, and was previously joking about my partner taking care of reproductive work while I take care of my research career. The conversation illustrates my shifting positions as a participant observer between researcher and a respectable middle-class young female:

> KATRINE: (…) if I was just here alone, I think it would be… lonely.
> AVIN: It would not be easy.
> SEHLA: It is much better [to have a family].
> KATRINE: But there is also a lot of family business to do. You know, I clean the family's house.
> AVIN: Here, everything is based on family.

> *KATRINE:* Washing the dishes, and 'Okay, now we have to go there, and now we have to go there.'
>
> *SEHLA:* Yeah, exactly. [*Laughter*]
>
> *KATRINE:* It is not my own will, it is just 'okay'! [*Laughter*]
>
> *SEHLA:* 'Okay, then I will come.' [*Laughter*]
>
> *KATRINE:* So, I will always bring necessary things, and a toothbrush in my bag because I never know where I am going to sleep. [*Laughter*]
>
> *AVIN:* That is right, here it [planning] is influenced.
>
> *SEHLA:* Yeah, exactly.
>
> *AVIN:* You know, at the moment I go home, I see my family: 'Oh, come to the car,' and then I am in my aunt's home. [*Sehla laughing*] It is just like that, you never plan. [*Laughter*]

In this excerpt, I move away from my position of researcher towards one of female family member by stressing my own experiences of family life in an attempt to share and match experiences with Sehla and Avin. In my dissertation, I point out how in this situation I negotiate my position in the field and position myself as someone who is also embedded in collective family decision-making. In hindsight, I will add that at the same time I took part in a performance of female respectability together with Sehla and Avin by stressing how I participate in reproductive housework; this is usually not something to mention specifically, so my vocalizing of it shows how in the conversation I am trying to hyper-perform as the right kind of helpful family member. I am trying to consolidate and get confirmation of my belonging to the social context. It generates a conversation around participating in middle-class family life as a collective movement by driving around in cars between different homes, but I will of course never know how Avin and Sehla would have talked about this had I not framed the conversation with my own presence. The conversation is an example of how I am trying to match and talk about experiences of local family life from the perspective of a young woman, a matching that would not have been possible if I had been there just as a researcher. I participated in these performances of respectability in continuously shifting positions on a sliding scale between knowing and not-knowing, partly outsider and partly insider, shifts that are always implicated in participant observation (Råheim *et al.* 2016, p. 4). These shifts can be understood as shifts between matching and mismatching with students. Maybe Avin and Sehla would have told me other things if I, in a different position as a more distanced researcher, had asked them about their everyday family life, and maybe we would not have discussed this kind of collective planning and reproductive work because I would not have thought about it had I not encountered it in my own embodied experience. I do not argue that the idea of a 'neutral' researcher would have produced better, more 'objective' knowledge. I am arguing that, to fully understand the subtext of the conversation, we also need to pay attention to the social situation and the fieldwork performances of both researcher and researched. There is no underlying 'truth' behind the performances; they are all there is, and we will not be able to know something more 'real' behind that. I am suggesting an analytical and methodological attention to desires and performances of attempted matching in fieldwork in order to get a rich understanding of what is going on and the knowledge that is produced from the specific social context. In the following, I shall look into how fieldwork performances create limits to knowing.

Unrespectable questions and answers: Fieldwork performances of gendered middle-class respectability

We were waiting for the elevator at the University of Sulaimani, Iraqi Kurdistan, after an interview. Xezal and Tara were female students at the Department of Education. Tara suddenly asked me if I had had a relationship (which I inferred as meaning a sexual one) with my partner before we got married. Or maybe it was not suddenly, but it felt like it, since I had no prior experience in this context of being asked questions about my relationship. I had just asked Tara a lot of questions myself, and now I felt the power of questioning in turn on my own body. I answered Tara that, yes, my partner and I had known each other as friends but that, most importantly, now we were married. What could I have learned from Tara about performances of gendered middle-class respectability (a central aspect of my object of study) if I had answered her question differently? What kind of conversations could that possibly have started if I had not closed down on talking about romantic and sexual relationships outside of marriage, what I automatically labelled as 'unrespectable behaviour'? And why was my performance of respectable marriage so important?

Upon arrival in Sulaimani in 2012, I had decided to visually perform a properly married heterosexual field persona, and I had bought a ring to symbolize the status of marriage. I had been in Sulaimani several times prior to this visit as a partner and family member without a ring. Starting the so-called fieldwork for my PhD research had made me take this decision (more on this below). When I waited for the elevator with Tara, I was confronted with my own performances of respectability. Sociologist Beverley Skeggs has worked on the concept of female respectability (Skeggs 1997). Drawing on Bourdieu's notion of habitus, Skeggs shows how English working-class women struggle with doing the right bodily performances and appearances in order to be perceived as respectable from the point of view of the scrutinizing middle-class gaze (Skeggs 1997). I felt caught in a kind of 'game' (Angrosino and Mays De Pe'rez in Råheim et al. 2016, p. 8) together with, especially, female students. A game of performing what I thought was the right kind of respectability that led to a closed door in terms of engaging in conversations outside of that script. My shying away from answering Tara's question about sexual relations before marriage was a detour to avoid the cracks in my respectability performance, which created tension and discomfort. Embodying the respectability, that I tried to study, hindered me in this situation from engaging with what could be labelled as 'unrespectable behaviour', and it hindered me from knowing. Tara's asking me a direct question also broke with my powerful position as the researcher being the one to ask the questions, thereby reversing the positions, and the question demanded of me to be accountable in private ways. This moment made it very clear to me how

I, without thinking deliberately about it, to some extent performed a specific kind of professional researcher in the field, and when this boundary was questioned I engaged in a respectability performance, which made me realize at a very embodied level how I, together with others, engage in these everyday performances all the time. When feeling a boundary being questioned, I saw and felt the whole game we were in together very clearly. I kept the door open to my own participation in an arena of respectability performances but closed it against getting to know more about the actual doings, and also instances of falling short, of this presumed shared gendered respectability. I realize now that my focus on being a respectable, correct version of myself as researcher actually made things weird, and I got stuck in a respectability trap with unanswerable questions that I could not engage in. This was not my plan, but it was the outcome. This hindered the analysis from going deeper because I myself stood in the way. Priyadharshini writes about coming 'unstuck' by arguing how '[u]nraveling the assumption of a coherent and stable identity for the researched also obliges the researcher's identity to come unstuck' (Priyadharshini 2003, p. 432). This means that the researcher does not 'arrive' in the field as a unified subject (Visweswaran in Priyadharshini 2003, p. 433), which points to a central tension in my research in that I performed and embodied a respectable gendered arrival in the field that I got absorbed into. I tried to hold together an impossible coherent subjectivity with which I could arrive smoothly in the field. This points to the difficulty of living and dealing with a post-structural theory of multiple selves in everyday life, as fieldwork is, and a slight slippage into a positivist ideal of the researcher as a person with a fixed subjectivity separate from what happens in the field. I was emerged in the field I was researching by participating in performances of gendered middle-classness, thereby becoming specific versions of myself in meetings with students in the concrete context. Following a post-structuralist Foucauldian understanding of the omnipresence of power, Priyadharshini suggests a methodological interest in nonstable and nonfixed positions for both researcher and researched, and a focus on 'the ways in which powerful individuals' multiple subjectivities are produced within the discourses in which they participate, and the points at which contradictions in those subjectivities arise' (Priyadharshini 2003, p. 429). In new future engagements with ethnographic fieldwork, I would try to be more attentive to my own grip of holding myself together as a coherent fixed researcher subjectivity that was evidenced here by my respectability performance. To truly give space to those kinds of reflections while engaging in research and writing up can be challenging when working at a fast academic pace. Linda Finlay stresses how a positivist hegemony still prioritizes what is perceived as the 'substantive story' over a reflexive account with the word limits in academic journals (Finlay 2002, p. 543). The question is then also what kind of support structures for early career researchers there are at universities. Inspired by Priyadharshini, I suggest using time and space to collectively explore how those weird, awkward moments of discomfort can come 'unstuck' so that we can learn something valuable from it. It appears that a focus on understanding how fieldwork performances by researcher and researched can both enable and stand in the way of knowing.

To dress up and paint a picture of oneself

> As feminist researchers, let us ask the question of what pictures of ourselves we are trying to paint and seriously consider how this informs our research decisions.
>
> (Whitson 2017, p. 305)

Risa Whitson discusses the balancing act between reflexivity around researcher subjectivity as self-indulgence and as an act that says something important about the research process and analysis. Whitson specifically reflects on how researcher subjectivity can be a matter of what she describes in the quote above as painting a picture of oneself. Writing about and engaging in fieldwork performances are intertwined and both aspects are part of the same reflexive manoeuvre where we present ourselves as researchers. When I engaged in fieldwork, I dressed up and presented myself in a certain way. I was wearing a dark-blue jacket for days when going to campus, to look more 'professional'. Students, especially, at the American University were very dressed-up in my eyes. Most female students at both universities wore quite a lot of make-up. I usually did not, but I made an effort with mascara. I did not in any way succeed in looking like the very well-dressed students, but going to the campuses was part of my social life, and I felt that an attempt to slightly match the dress code would help me fit in. My aim was that students would want to hang out with me during lunch in relation to my research, but I also wished just to match, be liked and to somehow fit in since this was also to be my everyday life for several months. I wrote in an email to my supervisor: 'Never have I had such an opportunity to cultivate a feminine look with styling, outfits, make-up and hair' (email 21 October 2012). It felt to me almost like 'dressing in drag' to conform to a certain kind of heterosexual femininity.

The decision to wear a ring was part of dressing up in my fieldwork performance. I had gone to the bazaar (the marketplace in the city centre) to find a pair of silver rings to make sure that my relationship looked 'right'. I was performing a partial act of being what Meera Sehgal symbolically describes as a 'veiled' researcher by hiding aspects of my identity (Sehgal 2009, p. 12). In my notebook, I wrote:

> I have bought a ring, and I remember to put it on my left hand's ring finger most days before I go out of the door. I make myself understandable as a married woman, not sure if it makes a big difference, but maybe in my own head.
>
> (Fieldnotes, Sulaimani, October 2012)

My notes underline the fact that I was the one who cared about that ring, and that I tried to control how I was perceived by others. This attempt to control was linked to my preconceptions regarding how others might think about me in the city and based on my knowledge of the generally accepted standard of couples who live together before marriage. One side of this picture was to visibly wear a symbol of marriage that felt important for me to signal when moving around on my own in taxis. And the other was that I envisioned being perceived as a proper adult, a body that could be read as a professional university employee doing 'serious research'. I had previous experiences in general of being perceived as a young student rather than a researcher, based on my gender and age, since I did not embody the classic image of research authority. Trying to pass as a 'proper researcher' stands in contradiction to the idea of studying sideways and trying to match with students, which shows my shifting positions as a researcher. In the whole process of gaining access to the university campuses through formal meetings with university staff, I wanted to be taken seriously and signal 'proper research'. When thinking about it now, it might just as easily have been my young student look that gave me official access to carry out research at both campuses. I met a fellow graduate student in Sulaimani who was also interested in gaining access to AUIS but had not succeeded. To me, he better fitted the image of a real grown-up adult, and like the 'proper' figure of a European male researcher. I wonder if my performance of respectable young female researcher in gender studies positioned me as a somewhat innocent researcher to have running around on campus and whether that helped me gain access. I can only guess. So much for the pictures that we try to paint of ourselves that end up being outside our control.

Priyadharshini writes about studying within academia and stresses how the terms of which kinds of access are granted to fields also shape the research (Priyadharshini 2003, p. 421). This is important in terms of understanding the power structures that we are operating in as researchers and researched. My access to the university institutions played a role in defining the 'field' I was studying. I did not just meet young people in town or in their homes; I met them as students in an institution that had granted me permission to be there. I was very cautious not to hang out with lecturers and staff, in order to stay as much as possible on the same level as students and clearly signal that I was interested in talking with them and keeping what we talked about to just amongst ourselves.

Using or telling the self

Moving from fieldwork to analysis, a way for me to try to nuance how ideas of respectability played out in the social arena was to clearly situate myself in the context and show in the analysis how I too performed respectability, so that I did not write a text about everybody else's concern about this respectability that I clearly also cared about myself. In my thesis, I was in some sections inspired by autoethnographic writing to make myself visible as the researcher where I found my situatedness to be relevant for the analysis. The autoethnographic writing of the researcher into the text both shows how knowledge is produced by a certain embodied researcher, but it is at the same time also a specific representation of the researcher in the text. One example of this is the elevator scene that I also included in my thesis, but I did not dig deeper into it – in a way, I closed off in order to present myself as a proper scholar in the text. This shows that we do not only perform as researchers in the field, but also in the representations of ourselves that we create in the text more or less explicitly. Another example of how I wrote myself into the text was related to trying to understand how having a car of one's own was connected to the performance of middle-classness. I did not hold a driver's licence, so I got into the routine of taking a taxi to the university campus in the morning. But a worry from family members about my moving around on my own led to a decision by my partner and myself to rent a car. Some days, my partner would drive me to campus, and on other days, I still took a taxi. I wrote about this in my thesis:

> [W]ith the rent of a car we became credible as a respectable middle-class couple moving around within the boundaries of 'safe spaces'. I just did not tell anybody when I behaved otherwise. Maybe people knew anyway, but this was an agreeable compromise settling the issue, keeping on the track of respectability.
>
> (Scott 2018, p. 184)

This embodied experience made me aware of the way cars are a class marker and a respectable and 'safe' way of moving around in the city. In the text, I did not just stay with my own experience as described above, but dug deeper into experiences of gendered and classed mobility among students.

Whitson, with experience from the field of human geography, points out the tension between reflexivity around researcher subjectivity as part of the research and as self-indulgence (Whitson 2017, p. 301). The risk of writing about oneself in the text is to end up spending too much time on the researcher and less on the researched. Skeggs, from a sociological perspective, is critical towards an over-emphasis on the researcher writing about herself, and she argues that reflexivity should focus on research practice and research participants (Skeggs 2002, p. 303). Skeggs states that '[t]he telling of the self becomes a manifestation and maintenance of difference and distinction' (Skeggs 2002, pp. 303–304). Anthropologist Anna Lærke, on the other hand, points out how she has written her own experience into the writing up of research in classrooms in the UK on the regulation of children's bodies (Lærke 2008). In an attempt to 'relinquish the power of ethnographic authority' (Lærke 2008, p. 145) she provides information to the reader about the specific person writing the text:

> Explicitly and deliberately using my self as a methodological tool became my way of making sense of emotional entanglement. Finding a respectable balance between navel-gazing and personally grounded intellectual curiosity is not easy – but neither is it impossible.
>
> (Lærke 2008, pp. 144–145)

Making visible the situatedness of knowledge production (Haraway 1988), where the researcher's embodied and always partial view is made visible, treads a fine line between Lærke's 'personally grounded intellectual curiosity' and Skeggs' critique of 'telling the self' as a manifestation of difference. My practical everyday and analytical engagement with middle-classness as the point from where I have been writing, that I have tried to make visible, carries a tension with a tradition of colonial anthropology where the European researcher is centred as the only knowing subject. While the methodological attempt to study sideways values students' experiences and narratives, I am in the end responsible as the author and storyteller of the specific piece of text that was examined as my thesis. As researchers, we are always framing and co-constructing narratives and experiences in the field. I believe it is honest and transparent to show how we are embedded in the fields we research to make it visible how we, both as researchers and researched, are positioned in various ways. My own partial view from a middle-class position was shaping how I understood and listened to students' experiences. What I herein describe as an attempted manoeuvre and wish to 'study sideways' was also connected to meeting students as individuals with agency, and not as a predefined vulnerable group. My focus was to meet students at eye level in the same way as if I had engaged in research with students in Copenhagen (Denmark) or Lund (Sweden), whom I would not have predetermined as a specifically vulnerable group and hence with a direction of 'studying down'. What I am reflecting on here is that this attempt to meet sideways in the category of studentness – inspired by Jette Kofoed's concept of pupilness (2008) with a focus on the doings of the category of pupil – and middle-classness risks overlooking all the contextual differences outside of these categories.

Reflecting on my research process and writing, in retrospect I see how I have at moments practised what I could name as a *mirroring of sameness* through inserting my own embodied research persona into the performances of middle-classness that I was analyzing, with the risk of overstressing sameness, such as universalizing what it means to be a university student, and what it entails to have middle-class aspirations. Heidi J. Nast uses the mirror metaphor to critique the ugly process of how difference is produced when defining oneself as different from the 'other' through a reflection in the 'other' as a passive surface (cited in Skeggs 2002, p. 6). Turning that imagery around, the idea of mirroring sameness might in other ways leak difference through moments of mismatching. When I avoided meeting Tara's question frankly, I upheld an assumed common respectability but without the possibility to get it confirmed and nuanced. At the same time, I upheld a specific presumed difference between life in Copenhagen and Sulaimani that was not tested or verified. My attempt to fit in to what I perceived as correct behaviour left certain conversations (in this case regarding romantic relationships and sexuality) unable to be explored in all their complexities – the non-existent conversations reifying presumed unspoken differences. In the analysis, even when the telling of my own embodied performances of female respectability was a way to analytically grasp what was going on from a wider perspective, it still produced difference and distinction despite the belief of a mirroring of sameness and a determinedness to study sideways.

Conclusion: Unravelling the stitches

I argue that the concepts of studying up, down and sideways are not fixed categories, but complex and shifting and show the limits and possibilities in ethnographic fieldwork. Participating in transnational research questions simple and fixed ideas of being able to clearly define what is up, down and sideways in terms of power relations between researcher and researched. The directions of up, down and sideways pertain not only to power relations but also to questions of difference and sameness. Studying sideways presumes a certain amount of recognizability and sameness between researcher and researched. Looking back, I describe the study that I have been engaged in as a complex, unstable and often failing kind of sideways across geographical and political contexts. This methodological approach opens up possibilities of capturing/seeing/analyzing global patterns of middle-classness, but at the same time risks creating unobserved areas in terms of unequal Global South–North relations. On the one hand, I argue for a critical reflection on how research can become stuck in narrow ideas of sameness, but I also want to expand on the concept of sideways and of whether something is the same or similar.

When I was asked the question 'If they are just like us, why should we read about them?' at the seminar, it touched on an important discussion of how to perceive, represent and analyze commonalities and differences, and how to develop critical and complex academic thought collectively that questions colonial structures in knowledge production. Revisiting my irritation at this type of question has made me better understand my own methodological approach.

Inspired by an image of a patchwork, I have been examining the methodological stitches that my research project was made of both in terms of fieldwork performances and reflexivity around my own position in the analysis. Several years later, it is much easier for me to look at that specific version of myself in time and place and see what was going on, and reflect further on the methodology used in my thesis. In this chapter, I have reflected on middle-classness, and especially respectability, as a research object in between the movement of holding together and coming undone. I have tried to show points of holding together in order to enable them to come undone. It takes time to release the tight grip of holding researcher and researched subjectivities together. Inspired by Priyadharshini's picture of 'coming unstuck', I imagine loosening the fabric that is sewn together in the patchwork so that there is space to breathe. The process of writing reflexively and allowing the tight grip to loosen, and putting on display the undone, is a productive research vulnerability that can make us think deeper and do better. By engaging with vulnerable reflections on fieldwork and analysis, we can pinpoint the preconceptions, expectations, social structures and power relations that we face and must navigate as researchers and researched. I argue for vulnerability in writing as a force for analytically grasping our positions in unequal global power structures and letting research be less of a sealed ready-package where we cannot learn from mistakes, problematic experiences and the moments of discomfort that these cause. When the economy of universities is based on productivity, including the ability of PhD students to finish their research on time, seminars where drafts are discussed become by default more focused on how to ask questions that are possible to answer and how to answer them in ways that will not delay the research process. Explorations of moments of discomfort, which become sidelined (partly due to the fast pace of academia), open to a reflexive self-investigation of how we as researchers are participating in fieldwork performances embedded in power structures. To create space for the production of this kind of reflexive knowledge, and to engage in vulnerable conversations about how to learn from the failures experienced, has transformative potential to think and do research in new ways. Time and space to engage in this ongoing reflexive process is crucial as it is never a quick fix to dwell on and try to learn from our moments of discomfort and failures in order to continually do better.

References

Bowman, D., 2009. *Studying up, down, sideways and through: Situated research and policy networks.* *The Future of Sociology: Proceedings of the Annual Conference of the Australian Sociology Association.* Canberra, Australia. Available from: https://www.gong.hr/media/uploads/bowman,_dina.pdf.

Butler, J., 1990. *Gender trouble: Feminism and the subversion of identity.* New York, NY; Oxford: Routledge.

Dirik, D., 2014. *Western fascination with "badass" Kurdish women.* Al Jazeera, last modified October 29, 2014, accessed March 28, 2021. https://www.aljazeera.com/opinions/2014/10/29/western-fascination-with-badass-kurdish-women.

Düvell, F., Triandafyllidou, A. and Vollmer, B., 2009. Ethical issues in irregular migration research in Europe. *Population Space and Place*, 16 (3), 227–239. doi:10.1002/psp.590.

Finlay, L., 2002. "Outing" the researcher: The provenance, process, and practice of reflexivity. *Qualitative Health Research*, 12 (4), 531–545. doi:10.1177/104973202129120052.

Gunaratnam, Y., 2003. *Researching race and ethnicity: Methods, knowledge and power.* London; Thousand Oaks; New Delhi: SAGE.

Haraway, D., 1988. Situated knowledges: The science question in feminism and the privilege of partial perspective. *Feminist Studies*, 14 (3), 575–599.

Hirshfield, L.E. and Ramahi, R., 2018. *Studying sideways: An ethnographic study of graduate students in chemistry.* SAGE Research Methods Cases. doi:10.4135/9781526444844.

hooks, b., 2015[1992]. *Black looks: Race and representation.* 2nd ed. London; New York: Routledge.

Kofoed, J., 2008. Appropriate pupilness: Social categories intersecting in school. *Childhood: A Global Journal of Child Research*, 15 (3), 415–430.

Lacy, K., 2019. The missing middle class: Race, suburban ethnography, and the challenges of "studying up". *Urban Ethnography: Legacies and Challenges. Research in Urban Sociology*, 16, 143–155.

Lærke, A., 2008. Confessions of a downbeat anthropologist. In: H. Ambruster and A. Lærke, eds. *Taking sides. ethics, politics, and fieldwork in anthropology.* New York, NY; Oxford: Berghahn.

Nader, L., 1972. Up the anthropologist: Perspectives gained from studying up. In: D. Hymes, ed. *Reinventing anthropology.* New York, NY: Pantheon Books, 284–311.

Plesner, U., 2011. Studying sideways: Displacing the problem of power in research interviews with sociologists and journalists. *Qualitative Inquiry*, 17 (6), 471–482. doi:10.1177/1077800411409871.

Priyadharshini, E., 2003. Coming unstuck: Thinking otherwise about "studying up". *Anthropology & Education Quarterly*, 34 (4), 420–437.

Råheim, M. et al., 2016. Researcher-researched relationship in qualitative research: Shifts in positions and researcher vulnerability. *International Journal of Qualitative Studies on Health and Well-Being*, 11 (1). doi:10.3402/qhw.v11.30996.

Scott, K., 2018. Seeking middle-classness: University students in Iraqi Kurdistan. PhD dissertation, Department of Gender Studies, Lund University, Lund, Sweden.

Sehgal, M., 2009. The veiled feminist ethnographer: Fieldwork amongst women of India's Hindu Right. In: M. Glebbeek and M. Huggins, eds. *Women fielding danger: Negotiating ethnographic identities in field research.* Boulder, MD: Rowman & Littlefield.

Skeggs, B., 1997. *Formations of class and gender – becoming respectable.* London; Thousand Oaks; New Delhi: SAGE.

Skeggs, B., 2002. Techniques for telling the reflexive self. In: T. May, ed. *Qualitative research in action.* London; Thousand Oaks; New Delhi: SAGE.

Whitson, R., 2017. Painting pictures of ourselves: Researcher subjectivity in the practice of feminist reflexivity. *The Professional Geographer*, 69 (2), 299–306. doi:10.1080/00330124.2016.1208510.

6

DILEMMAS OF REPRESENTATION IN A STUDY OF SOCIAL WORKERS

Analyzing non-evident forms of social transformation

Vanna Nordling

Prologue: The theme of my thesis

> …it just has to be that one gets to know a youth, and then they become a Dublin case[1] and they are to be deported… and who sends youth [back] to Malta or Italy? Who can sleep well after doing that? If you have heard these accounts, what they have gone through, there is not a chance. And you can't just say, 'Well, go somewhere else and hide' either, so it becomes a responsibility: what the hell should I do?[2]

In the quote, a social worker describes her reaction when some of the young persons she is meeting through her work are to be deported. They tell her about experiences of violent border controls, as well as other traumatic experiences, and she argues that her awareness of these gives her a responsibility: she needs to act upon the situation. In this case, the social worker helps some of the young persons to avoid Swedish authorities, something that goes clearly beyond her job specification. In an interview study of social workers within the Swedish welfare state who actively had been giving support to young people risking deportation, I analyzed such experienced responsibility and the dilemmas that it brought up (Nordling 2017).[3] Central to the analysis was a tension between *actions* reaffirming the status quo and *acts* calling for the recognition of rights claims based on ideas of justice (Isin 2008). I argued that the social workers' support was maybe not changing the system, but that it could be understood as destabilizing ideas of responsibility and of who is included in a community. My analysis discussed how to understand forms of social transformation that are not straightforward; the social workers were *both* a part of oppressive structures *and* made efforts to challenge these same structures, and it was sometimes problematic to bring these nuances forward in the analysis.

Introduction: Discomfort of representation

But why social workers? Aren't they the ones taking the children from immigrants?

The question above was asked at my dissertation. I perceived it as a friendly question aiming at reflexive discussion, but it wasn't the first time I'd received this kind of comment in an academic setting.[4] This has made me reflect upon how my study was perceived and understood: is it possible to write about social workers giving support to persons risking deportation in a way that still takes the exclusionary tendencies of the welfare state into account? Presenting an analysis that fronted the accounts of social workers was a balancing act due to their power position in relation to the youth to whom they were giving support. They were employed within a welfare state organization that was experienced as exclusionary by many of its service users. Their support to the youth did not lead to social transformation, in the sense of making fundamental changes in society (Khondker and Schuerkens 2014), and often their support was arbitrary. When giving support there is, generally, a complex relation between 'helper' and 'helped', where the 'helper' has the power to decide who is 'deserving' of support (Panican and Ulmestig 2016). Therefore, social work practice, even if supportive at an individual level, often reinforces the present relations of power. At the same time, the social workers whom I interviewed went beyond what was formally expected of them, and their support could be understood as a form of resistance to exclusions; this created a tension that caught my interest.

Like many critical theorists, I saw, and still see, knowledge and action not as separate but as linked together: with this perspective, the researcher must be concerned with the consequences of knowledge (Dant 2003; see also Introduction in this volume). As a participant in social movements, I was well aware of the ambivalence inherent in most efforts to create systemic transformation that at the same time use the (almost always) insufficient means at hand.[5] I drew on my experiences from the Swedish No Border movement, where the tension between humanitarian aid meeting urgent needs but not challenging the border regime, and more far-reaching critiques of the system through campaigns and other forms of activism, were discussed and problematized at the time of writing my thesis (Sager 2015). I recognized this tension in the social workers' accounts. My interest in the social workers' practices was hence less about finding a case that would neatly illustrate a theoretical point than about searching for tools that could help me to explore complex and often contradictory ways of trying to transform society through everyday practice. I found that this kind of practice could sometimes be difficult to place into a theoretical framework: there was too much ambivalence and I couldn't analyze the support as *either* resistance *or* oppression.

My selection criterion had been social workers crossing their professional boundaries in order to give support to persons risking deportation, and initially I didn't focus on diversity in this group. However, the study's participants were diverse, for example, as to age, gender and/or whether they were participating in social movements or not. Many of the social workers also had their own experience of migration, and they described how this affected their relationship to the youth. I have later realized that I didn't always make such experiences and differences visible in the analysis, as my research interest made me focus on social transformation and on the social workers' *practices*. Due to this focus as well as to concerns of anonymization, I presented the social workers by their professional titles. As I will discuss in more detail below, the professional title is often associated with 'neutrality' as well as whiteness, and this has made me wonder if my analysis would have been received differently if I had succeeded in providing a more nuanced representation. Would another way of representing the social workers, bringing their individual experiences to the fore, have made it easier to see their agency? Would I then have faced the same questions about social workers as potentially oppressive actors? What did my analysis bring forward and which starting points or assumptions made me perform it in the way I did? When making analytical choices, there might be unforeseen consequences, and this chapter is an attempt to reflect back upon, and learn from, this process.

The chapter focuses on ethics of representation and I discuss the balancing act between different views of social workers when 'writing up' the analysis. The representation of social workers as complex actors, neither 'doing good' nor only being repressive, on many occasions led to tensions and moments of discomfort when presenting my study. Therefore, the aim of the chapter is to analyze obstacles when trying to represent the social workers as complex actors who sometimes practise resistance while still being a part of exclusionary structures. After a brief presentation of social work in a Swedish context, where I highlight that social workers are often associated with neutrality and a supposedly 'good' welfare state, I reflect upon my analytical choices. I discuss the choices I made when representing the individual social workers in the analysis, especially the decision to present the research participants using their professional titles. This might have added to the idea of the 'neutral social worker', but it also helped me to focus on institutional conditions and the limits set by ideas of 'professionalism'. After that, I reflect upon what my theoretical lens allowed me to see, and what actually became a main focus in my analysis: the ambivalent relation between social work and activist ideals of social transformation. I identify a tension between social transformation and everyday practice that often was difficult to communicate to different audiences, but that helped me to constantly go back and reflect upon my material. I argue that the methodological dilemmas I faced, and the tensions I struggled with in terms of representations and different expectations from different audiences, actually brought the analysis forward.

Background: Social work and borders in a Swedish context

> Now, again we need to decide what Europe we want to be. My Europe welcomes people who flee from war, is solidary and united. My Europe doesn't build walls; we help each other when the need is great.
>
> And if we carry the mission together, we can make a difference for people. Sweden and Germany can't do it by ourselves. All EU countries must help.
>
> (Speech by Swedish Prime Minister Stefan Löfvén,
> Regeringskansliet 2015, my translation)

On 6 September 2015, Swedish Prime Minister Stefan Löfvén gave a speech that is often shown as an example of the government's first response to the increased number of people on the move who arrived in Sweden in 2015. In the speech, Löfvén expressed a view of Sweden as an open country, and as a country taking responsibility. During the following months, the official rhetoric rapidly changed into a story of 'crisis' and of a need for restrictive migration policies and closed borders. Only a year later Löfvén said in an interview that 'the combats in Mosul indicate a need for continued border controls' (Magnusson 2016, my translation), demonstrating a shift in priorities from the situation of people fleeing war zones to an idea of 'protecting' the Swedish borders.

The quote from September 2015 is in line with an image of Sweden as humanitarian and a conception of Sweden as an advanced welfare state (Martinsson *et al.* 2016). This was an important context for my study: when studying representatives of the Swedish welfare state one must, in one way or another, relate to these, deeply rooted, images. My interviews were performed before 2015, and at that time the idea of Swedish exceptionalism was less questioned than it is today – even though there were critical analyses of the erosion of the welfare state (Schierup and Ålund 2011), indicating that the changes in practice and rhetoric have been gradual. The strong connotations of the modern, 'good' and universal welfare state – an international reputation (Lister 2009) as well as a national self-image (Martinsson and Reimers 2020) – might lead the audience of my research to expect representations of welfare workers 'doing good'. Furthermore, in a Swedish context, social work as a profession has been developed in close relation with the formation of the welfare state, and most of the professionalized social work is practised by social workers employed by the Swedish municipalities. Social workers may within this context uncritically be perceived as neutral bureaucrats. This image can also be connected to ideas of whiteness. For example, ethnographer Sabine Gruber (2016, p. 95) shows how ideas of professionalism, in the sense of being able to represent the values of the

Swedish welfare state (such as gender equality), are tied to ideas of having a 'Swedish background', and hence to racialized ideas of who can perform certain work tasks.

Perhaps it is needless to say that the view of Sweden as generous and open was criticized by the No Border movement long before 2015.[6] There is also a longstanding academic tradition of studying social welfare institutions as markers of borders and boundaries separating citizens from non-citizens and producing hierarchies of 'deservingness', linked to colonialism and racism (Balibar 2004, Nyers 2008). In this context, it is crucial to bear in mind that social workers are in a position where they sometimes have a far-reaching power over people's lives. Social workers belong to one of the groups that are engaged in negotiations of the boundaries of citizenship, in relation to migrants' access to social services and benefits (Nordling 2017). A growing research literature, as well as accounts in news media and from activists, pinpoints the exclusionary aspects of the welfare state and the fear that certain (not least the racialized) populations experience in relation to the social services (Wikström 2013, Gruber 2016). As indicated in the initial quote in this text, fear of the social services in relation to child protection, and especially of losing one's child, is well-documented (Nordling et al. 2020). Moreover, persons with an irregularized status (residing as undocumented) often hesitate to contact social workers or other welfare state employees due to a fear of deportation (Hermansson et al. 2020). When, as in my study, focusing on social workers who actually give support to youth risking deportation, there is a risk of losing sight of such exclusionary tendencies. Along the way, I learned especially to underline the fact that the border is materialized in the encounters between the social services and persons lacking Swedish residency: in the decisions as to who is 'deserving' of support and through an ever-present risk of deportation.

In a Swedish context, it has been argued that the relatively inclusive welfare state has led to a stronger focus on border enforcement (Hammar 1999). Irregularized migrants' access to welfare services has been limited, but in 2013, new laws were introduced giving irregularized children access to schooling and healthcare, and irregularized adults access to healthcare that cannot be deferred (Nielsen 2016). This shows that irregularized migrants' access to social rights was on the political agenda when my interviews took place. In the case of the social services, however, access to social rights such as food and housing has been more limited and disputed. The social workers in my study were expected to follow the decisions of the Swedish Migration Agency and to psychologically 'let go' of the young people they were working with in case they were denied asylum. At the same time, as I discussed in my study, there was sometimes also an access to rights – even if it was produced in contradictory and ambiguous ways, often marking new borders.

As argued by anthropologist Didier Fassin (2015), state institutions are not to be understood as neutral but as shaped through their agents, who make assessments and have feelings. Fassin (2015, p. 256) argues that 'the agents think and act simultaneously with what is said and done in the public sphere and the political world'. This street–level view of bureaucrats, which opens up for seeing individual agency, has been important to my understanding of social workers. In a Swedish context, social workers' closeness to welfare state institutions seems to make it more difficult to openly challenge these same institutions. Studies have shown that social workers are afraid of voicing protest and that they express a fear of being seen as unprofessional by their colleagues and also of negative reactions or reprisals (Hedin *et al.* 2009, Lauri 2016). Instead, in many cases the protests are of a more silent character, indicating that social workers' protests need to be assessed in other ways than when studying public forms of protest. For instance, ways to express protest have been through anonymous blog posts (NBTV 2015) or through performing social work in the 'borderlands' between the welfare state organizations and civil society activism (Aracena 2015, p. 187).

Focusing on the complexity and ambiguity of street-level bureaucrats, I understand social workers as *both* affected by established power relations and racist discourses *as well as* by ideas of resistance. The social workers in my study were confronting borders in their everyday work, and this sometimes led to new understandings of what was a responsible way of acting. They acted upon these understandings in various ways, *both* reaffirming *and* challenging oppressive relations of power, something that I discuss in more detail in the sections below.

Dilemmas of disembodied representation

> More often than not research findings are presented in the form of long block of quotations from research respondents. These excerpts are expected simply to speak for themselves. The portraits of research participants are sketched lightly if at all and the social location of the respondent lacks explication and contextual nuance. Sociological data is reduced to a series of disembodied quotations.
>
> (Back 2007, p. 17)

In social science research, presenting research findings usually means representing research participants in certain ways (Pickering and Kara 2017). For instance, my interpretations need to be balanced with research participants' concerns and ethics of anonymization. At the time of writing my analysis, the concern that I felt most acutely was *what* I could tell, due to research ethics. The social workers did things that were against their work instructions, such as giving support outside of work or bringing persons who risked deportation to their private homes. Many of the social workers feared that there would be reprisals (to themselves or general limitations to support practices) if their practices were known of, and I felt that the ways in which I could present the material such that they would be acceptable to the participants were limited. I have afterwards reflected on whether, and how, this might have led to my making 'disembodied quotations' (Back 2007, p. 17) strengthening the image of neutral and disembodied social workers – and hence possibly undermining my argument that social workers need to be understood in context. In this section, I therefore discuss a practical dilemma when writing up: how to picture the social workers as complex actors?

A central focus in my analysis was the idea of the 'neutral' professional versus that of an arbitrary support outside of the professional role. The social workers in my study reported having little power over their work situations and that they instead often acted within a sphere that could be described as 'private' when they chose to give support to the minors. This meant that the analysis could not be entirely based on the social workers acting as welfare state representatives. At the same time, the professional role was central to my interviews, as the social workers came into contact with the youth through their work, and this fact set the limits for what was possible to do openly. In my thesis, I argued that the acts in support of the minors could in many cases be placed in a space 'in between' the professional role and a private sphere. The position of the social workers was not being *either* welfare state representatives *or* private persons, and their acts were affected by a power position within the welfare state *as well as* by resistance to this position. In order to detect the space 'in between', I found it important to bring the professional role and the expectations that this role implied to the fore.

The social workers in my study described an expectation from colleagues and managers to keep a psychological distance from the minors. This was often connected to an idea of the professional social worker as 'neutral' and, thereby, that the social worker should not get too personally involved with the client. For example, one of the study's participants told me that her activism in the asylum rights movement was an issue that she did not wish to bring up with her managers or colleagues:

> ...the asylum rights movement was something that you almost should not talk about, I felt. And you could think that it should be a merit to be involved in the asylum rights movement, because you work with the children and then you get more insights in... you can help them in different ways. But I experienced that it was nothing positive, more the other way around. Then it [the asylum rights movement activism] was suddenly a commitment without boundaries and that it would maybe be easier to commit misconduct.

As the quote illustrates, the social worker was perceived as being 'too committed' by managers and/or colleagues. Listening to the social workers, I learned that many of them worried about how their accounts in the interviews would be received when my work was published. During the interviews we therefore discussed what matters could be seen as sensitive. In order to avoid disclosing such things, I chose not to focus on details in the social workers' accounts. For example, I often avoided quotes where workplaces or work routines were described in particular depth. Even when I included general comments on the support being far-reaching and against the work instructions, I didn't go into detail. Instead of focusing on exactly *what* they did, my main focus in the analysis was on how the practices could be understood. For example, when analyzing how a social worker invited a former 'client' to live with her as a way to avoid deportation, my focus was much less on her story than on how the act could be interpreted (i.e. if it was divergent or not). In this way, the tension between social transformation and reaffirming the status quo, the aspect that interested me, became more visible, although at the cost of losing individual accounts.

Another, related, concern was anonymization. As the social workers feared reprisals, I found it to be of special importance to tell their stories in a way that would not be possible to trace to individual social workers. My solution at the time was to anonymize the social workers, calling them only by their work titles (social assistant, personnel at accommodation centre, guardian) and to present their accounts thematically. I let the participants speak to each other, instead of following one person at a time, and various voices were combined. I sometimes did discuss aspects of age, gender and of sharing language and/or migration background with the youth, but this was not a main focus in the analysis. This way of presenting the social workers, of course, had consequences for the analysis (compare Kolankiewicz's chapter in this volume). Was it enough to *state* that some of the social workers had their own experiences of flight, and even of residing as undocumented, when it wasn't focused on in the analysis? The anonymization to some extent obscured the fact that the social workers had diverse backgrounds and made the reader instead focus on their, seemingly 'neutral', work titles. This image could easily feed into the image of social workers as distant from the social worlds of their 'clients'. A professional title following each quote risked reinforcing the expectations of neutrality. It may also have underlined the assumption of a distant and white social worker, as no clear counter-image was presented. And if some stories are reinforced, other stories risk being obscured. If ideas of 'professionalism', 'neutrality' and whiteness are already attached to the image of the social worker, then what room for manoeuvre is there to picture social workers who do not fit into this image? Because there were indeed other stories among the study's participants. One example among many was a social worker at an accommodation centre who told me that her migrant background affected her relationship to the youth:

> Of course you get closer. They call me 'aunt', for example; they don't say that to the others – the others are personnel [...], so of course it's – I get warm inside, it's really tender to say that, instead of saying 'you', or call my name…

Even if I did discuss this quote in my thesis, the general focus of the analysis risked rendering such accounts, and hence the plurality among the social workers, invisible. It also, maybe more importantly, risked missing how responsibility can be mobilized in different ways depending on where the social worker is situated in relation to hierarchies based on race and/or the construction of national boundaries. Anonymizing the social workers hence affected how I could make their acts understandable.

Taking the representations of participants seriously, and balancing the analysis with the participants' concerns, has been described as a central challenge of representation – a challenge that underlines the need for reflexive research (Pickering and Kara 2017). After finishing my thesis, I have reflected upon what consequences my concern with anonymization had for the representation. If performed differently, my study could have contributed to a more nuanced picturing of the research participants. I chose to centre their position within the *welfare state*, but a deeper understanding of the social workers' backgrounds could have informed a more multidimensional analysis regarding their position in relation to the *nation state* and ideas of 'Swedishness'. To tell the social workers' stories would have made it more difficult to anonymize, but it would indeed have brought other dimensions to the analysis and increased the understandings as to why the social workers did what they did.[7]

When reflecting back on my analysis, I realize that there were perspectives that I didn't see and questions that I neglected to ask. However, this text is not to be read as an effort to 'make it right'; rather, it is an attempt to critically discuss my study in order to learn from it. The project of nuancing the image of social workers and understanding their acts in relation to their own positions and experiences would indeed have given my analysis a different focus, but it would also probably have taken the focus from the tension between *actions* reaffirming the status quo and *acts* challenging it that interested me in the first place. Instead of individual representations, my analysis focused on what the social workers had in common: the practices of support to the youth from a position within the welfare state. This had been my selection criterion and it was what mainly interested me: the ambivalence in their acts, the balancing between the welfare state and civil society activism, the possible renegotiations of the welfare state in spaces 'in between'.

My analysis focused on the (generalized) *practices* of the social workers, rather than on their positionalities. It thereby, to some extent, separated act from actor in order to make another analytical point. This may have made it more difficult to see the social workers beyond images of 'neutrality' or 'good welfare state employees', but it also facilitated a certain form of analysis that focused on practice instead of person: in order to study certain things, others were left out. Therefore, at the time of doing my analysis, I found that it made sense to present the social workers' professional titles rather than giving more situated and personal accounts. The titles could give the reader a hint of what kind of organizational limitations the social workers were facing – for example, a social assistant, making decisions on housing and schooling from her office, had a formalized role that made it difficult to give far-reaching support within the limits of what was seen as 'professional'. On the other hand, the social assistant had more space to act in support of the minor during her time off – a time that was divided from work hours in a much clearer way than in the case of social workers at accommodation centres for unaccompanied minors, who worked close to the everyday life of the youth but who were often advised not to contact the youth during their time off. The decision to focus on professional titles hence helped me to include the institutional conditions in my analysis and to highlight what was formally at stake for the different categories of social workers: it permitted me to see something that might have been obscured by another analytical lens. Instead of picturing the social workers as potentially close to their 'clients', the analysis centred on their *role as social workers*. It follows that one answer to the question 'why social workers?' would be that 'social workers are interesting *because of* their ambivalent position of power at the boundaries of the welfare state', and not because social workers are 'good' or that they, as a profession, would oppose deportations.

In the next section, I reflect upon what my theoretical lens allowed me to see, and what actually became a main focus in my analysis: the ambivalent relation between social work and activist ideals of social transformation.

Representing social workers' dual positions

> The work we do is in solidarity with those crossing the border and living without papers in the United States, but our grief is not necessarily in solidarity; our grief is our own. I grieve the loss I feel when I part ways with someone in the desert, and the pain I feel because murderous politics permit mass graves and deport people I know. I grieve when I come across bones in the desert that turn out to be human, although my sorrow is inherently different than that of the family of the person I've found.
>
> (Sandusky 2017)

In this quote, Lee Sandusky from the organization No More Deaths • No Más Muertes describes her grief from the position of an activist – trying to do what she can to support people crossing the border between Mexico and the United States, but knowing that she can never do enough. This ambivalent position of grieving social suffering and at the same time facing the power position inherent in the act of, as a citizen, giving support to persons who become irregularized through harsh migration policies is at the heart of many forms of migrants' rights activism (see Söderman's chapter in this volume). As an activist in the Swedish No Border movement, with its inherent contradictions of, on the one hand, wanting to transform the system and, on the other hand, trying to make the present system accept individual asylum claims, I was interested in investigating the social workers' dual positions of trying to act for social transformation while also being a part of a welfare state organization. My interest in the social workers' support to the youth was hence related to my activism. Although this helped me to identify, and partly understand, the social workers' ambivalence, it led to difficulties: as I was positioned close to the social workers I risked taking things for granted. I also felt uncomfortable when being identified with the social workers, as their support to the youth often simultaneously reinforced exclusions and categorizations that I found to be problematic. In this section, I will therefore reflect upon what became a central interest for me in the analysis and what I tended to centralize rather than a representation of the social workers' positionalities: the tension between wishing for structural transformation while also being attentive to individual needs. I will discuss how this tension led to ambivalent forms of transformation that I struggled to make visible in the analysis.

An important dimension that brought tensions to the analysis was the relationship between 'helper' and 'helped'. Much of the critique of helping practices takes a starting point in the critique of humanitarian aid. As a universalist ethic, humanitarianism has the idea of a common humanity and has been implemented in international law. A growing body of literature, however, shows that humanitarianism serves as a depoliticizing factor (Fassin 2007, Ticktin 2011). Some authors describe how an image of migrants as victims is replacing the image of the rights-bearing refugee (Ticktin 2011). In a much-quoted text, Didier Fassin (2007, p. 500) describes humanitarian action as a 'politics of life': there is a radical inequality underlying humanitarian aid in that humanitarian organizations can decide which lives should be saved and which lives could be risked. Such critiques are valid also in the area of social work, with its inherent power relations between 'helper' and 'helped'. As most Swedish social workers are also welfare state representatives, this issue became even more complicated than if I had interviewed activists who were more openly opposing the exclusionary sides of the welfare state. Even though there are ideals of social transformation connected to social work as a profession (e.g., Ferguson 2007), it was difficult for the social workers in my study to openly follow other logics than the organizational – a logic that kept the status quo. This meant that the social workers whom I interviewed were facing a situation where they didn't feel that they could do what was best for the youth and at the same time act in accordance with the organizational protocol. The tension between 'managing law' and being a 'fellow human being' has been described as inherent to Swedish social work (Kamali 2015), and it was salient in many of my interviews. Having to balance between the 'neutral' professional and the 'compassionate' fellow human being created a complexity and ambiguity among the social workers: a duality that was different from the position of an activist within a social movement.

When performing my analysis, I was interested in ambiguities in relation to social transformation, and I wanted to analyze transformation that was not straightforward. As described above, this interest was also rooted in my participation in social movements. I therefore turned to theorists exploring everyday resistance to present citizenship regimes (Isin 2008, 2012, McNevin 2012). These theories helped me to pinpoint that inclusion and exclusion are not fixed, but negotiated through practice. I understood the social workers' support to young people risking deportation as *destabilizing* ideas of rights and responsibilities in relation to the welfare state: a main focus in my analysis was how different forms of acts could potentially, and often temporarily, destabilize the status quo. As exemplified by one of the social workers who worked at an accommodation centre for unaccompanied minors:

> I haven't been politically active, it hasn't been… But everything becomes political in that I oppose how the system is run.

In the quote, the social worker reflected upon how she would understand her own acts. She had begun to see her acts as 'political' because she was doing things that were in opposition to what was expected of her at the workplace. In this case, the reflection concerned a situation where her colleagues expected neutrality and distance, but where she had instead chosen to invite a young person to live in her home in order to avoid a deportation. She acted upon another logic than was expected of her and she understood her responsibility in new ways. This was one of the ways in which I understood 'destabilizations' in my analysis.

At the same time, the social workers' support was often based on relationships to specific minors as well as on ideas of 'compassion'. The support given was often ambivalent and not always directed towards social justice; it could therefore also be dismissed as a form of 'humanitarian' support without any transformative potential. In my analysis, however, I saw how ideas of social transformation could intersect with ideas of 'compassion' and how the encounters with youth risking deportation could make the social workers think in new ways. For instance, one of the social workers in my study told me:

> You know, I want you to know this: my friends are Sweden Democrats.[8] It is totally crazy what you have – in this area live people who believe in this way, and I have also; there was a time when I thought the same, I can honestly say that I have. Eh, what made me change my mind? I think it was when I started to teach these three youngsters, that's when I started to see it differently.

This quote illustrates a shift in understandings from a support of nationalist and far-right ideas to engaging profoundly in the everyday lives of youth with experience of migration, a transformation that the social worker describes as dependent on her meeting the boys face-to-face. New and more radical approaches may sometimes emerge from encounters with social suffering (e.g., Maestri and Monforte 2020), and change may hence come gradually. Also, just as other authors have noted, movements based on humanitarian ideals are often intersecting with more radical social movements (Sager 2015, Picozza 2017). This was something that I recognized in the accounts of the study's participants. My study was inspired by activist campaigns based on the idea that everyone has a responsibility to make a change: for example, campaigns asking employees of airline companies to refuse to deport people, or headmasters of elementary schools to welcome irregularized students (before the law change as described above). As expressed by activist and researcher Maja Sager (2011, p. 194):

> …the struggle to gain access on an individual level is often closely related to collective levels of struggle for access. For example, an indication of the way that engagement on the level of 'individual needs' tends to spill over into other forms of politics can be seen in the way representatives for the underground clinics have become important voices in asylum rights debate.

Thus seemingly individual acts could be understood as parts of a larger social movement, something that also my analysis brought to the fore. In that sense, a focus on possible destabilizations regarding who is a responsibility of the welfare state was also connected to research ethics, in the sense of doing research contributing to a politics of hope rather than dystopia (Martinsson and Mulinari 2018), yet without denying the new hierarchies and exclusions that may emerge when challenging present citizenship practices.

My analysis was triggered by the idea that social transformation may be contradictory; however, it seems like the same tension that triggered my curiosity was also causing a feeling of discomfort: I felt that the questions I received, such as 'why social workers?', indicated that I didn't make myself understandable as a critical researcher. As discussed above, to spotlight destabilizations and everyday acts of social transformation was in accord with views present in the social movements where I was based, and where my ideas were rooted, at the time of the study. Through my activist standpoint, I understood myself as having a critical position in relation to present border regimes – and this included an insight into the exclusionary sides of citizenship. Probably this was a point of departure that was so obvious to me that I didn't always think about making it evident to others. To participate in an activist movement could in this way have been a blind spot: I risked overlooking the need to contextualize and explain my standpoint as I was part of a context, both in academia and among my activist friends, where such critique was their own starting point. However, my position also allowed me to see the complexities of a practice that was *both* striving for structural changes and being attentive to social suffering. Taking part in a social movement, I was positioned close to some of the social workers in my study and I could recognize the duality in their practices. However, as I mention above, I did not always feel comfortable when I was identified with the social workers. Geographer Risa Whitson (2017) points to an important difference between describing one's position and one's subjectivity – the latter regarding the researcher's emotions and feelings of (dis)affiliation and/or (dis)comfort. According to Whitson, an investigation of researcher subjectivity means asking questions about who I want to be as a researcher and where I am at ease. For example, she suggests that research subjects living in the margins are more easily identified as 'appropriate subject[s] of critical feminist research' than other, more privileged, groups (ibid., p. 302). This, in turn, can be related to whom the researcher wishes to be. In my case, I realized that I found it important to identify with my study: it troubled me when I was seen as naïve or as someone who idealized the social workers – this was not whom I understood myself to be. My discomfort with the reactions to my study can be related to this identification: I wanted other critical researchers to understand me and see me as an ally. This was also a reason why I found it difficult to legitimize my study in relation to different academic audiences: the topic in itself gave rise to associations that I needed to address repeatedly. Still, the ambivalent position of the social workers was exactly what caught my interest in the first place. The feeling of being questioned also ultimately helped me forward, as I was forced to constantly go back and reflect upon my material. Paradoxically, the tension brought about by the position of the social workers, which I have discussed throughout this text, created fruitful frictions between my interviews and theoretical discussions in the analysis, but it was *also* one of the reasons for my discomfort.

Concluding remarks: Tensions that helped me forward

What slips out of my grasp, or is easily framed as someone else's bad habit? And yet, what is it that I might want to push away, but which continues to insist, keeps interrupting the neat narratives of self, theory, and politics I have a vested interest in?

(Hemmings 2018, pp. 7–8)

In this quote, Clare Hemmings, a leading scholar in gender studies, points to the importance of, and difficulty for, a researcher keeping to the questions that trouble them. This text has been an effort to critically discuss, but also to better understand, my analytical choices. There are many things that I could have done differently when 'writing up', and at the time of my study some of them were less visible to me than they are today. Going back and reflecting upon my analysis, I have learnt that it is difficult to address all issues at once, and that one analytical perspective – no matter how interesting it might be – easily obscures other perspectives and insights. This isn't necessarily a problem, but it might be a struggle to position oneself in relation to different academic fields and perspectives. I also have a responsibility towards the participants and the way in which the phenomenon that I study is contextualized. The representation takes place in a societal context that is changing and that may be difficult to grasp. What is easy to understand in one academic room might need more thorough explanation in another, and may be understood in yet another way in an activist context. Hence, despite being unable to avoid the question 'why social workers?', I can learn to better understand it, and thereby provide better answers.

My choice to represent the social workers in a way that could be described as 'disembodied' did not bring individual experiences of oppression to the fore, but it opened up other analytical possibilities. A central part of my analysis focused on how practice brings friction to theory, as practice is often complex and full of ambivalence: the social workers in my study were *both* reaffirming *and* challenging oppressive relations of power. My study focused on ambiguities in relation to social transformation and I wanted to analyze transformation that was not straightforward. The interest in the social workers' support was rooted in my activism, but it could still be difficult to discuss it in terms of social transformation. What we do – as social workers, as activists or as researchers – is not 'pure' and we cannot always foresee the consequences.

When writing this text and making an effort to learn from my methodological choices as well as from my choice of study subject, I have repeatedly come back to the fact that the *tensions* are what keep me going. The dilemmas of representation, both of individual social workers and of social work in a larger societal context, brought me forward in the analysis and helped me to analyze how everyday practices create friction in relation to theoretical, as well as political, ideals of social transformation. I believe that contradictions are almost necessarily created when trying to intervene in society, in contrast to more abstract forms of theorizing. To me, pointing to the tensions that arise, and making them visible, is a good starting point. This would mean a foregrounding of tensions in the analysis instead of seeking to resolve them. But it would also entail reflecting upon my own choices and assumptions, asking: where could I have gone more deeply; what questions did I overlook?

Epilogue: Changing border regimes, changing representations

We are tired now. Many of us burned out. Many with disastrous private economies. We are the welfare workers, the silver threads that the society is built of. We are needed. When we lose hope, you lose us. And it is about the now. Now many of us, who have been loyal to the construction of this society, are so disillusioned that we are no longer interested in bringing the society and the welfare system forward. Our work ethic is hollowed. Now our faith is disappearing.

(# vistårinteut 2019, my translation)

In an open letter to the Swedish Social Democrats, a network of welfare state professionals and volunteers, # vistårinteut [*vi står inte ut*: 'we can't stand it'], urges the politicians to listen to their demands for refugee amnesty and to their experiences of working with youth who are living in precarious circumstances due to Swedish migration policies. The letter was written in 2019, 5 years after I had finished doing my interviews. As the letter indicates, today social workers are organized together with other professionals and their (collective) opposition to Swedish migration policies is much more open than it was in 2014.

Over the passage of time, I have noticed that my project has received somewhat new, different responses following the present political development. In a context of even harsher migration policies since 2015, a range of welfare professionals have begun to speak up and protest against the effects of present policies in more open and direct ways than they did in my study (Martinsson and Reimers 2020). Evidently, more people are reacting along similar lines to the social workers whom I interviewed. As the frames have changed, the study's participants may, at least partially, be understood in the light of an emerging movement among professionals instead of as individual actors trying to 'do good'. According to geographer Engin Isin (2012), *duration* is not only the time it takes for an event to happen; events may be interpreted in new ways long after they have taken place. It is too early to tell where more outspoken conflicts concerning migration policies might lead. Maybe they won't lead to larger transformations or ruptures – but they seem to underline the idea of destabilizations of rights and responsibilities in relation to the welfare state. The openness of today's protests also makes it less risky to write about the different practices of the social workers in my study, as they are already outspoken and can be seen as one example among many others. But new contexts also bring new risks; the issue of social work in relation to persons who are denied asylum is today more politicized in a Swedish context (Persdotter and Nordling 2020 forthcoming), and therefore the topic might be more debated when made visible today. Social workers who engage in open protests might be perceived as having a more critical, and thereby potentially more threatening, position in relation to the welfare state than the ones performing silent acts, unnoticed by colleagues and managers.

Over the last 10 years, the Swedish No Border movement has also increasingly begun to question categorizations such as (citizen) 'activists' and 'migrants' (Nordling *et al.* 2017), making way for possible new understandings of agency and giving support – and hence questioning the distinction between 'helper' and 'helped'. A context of a more outspoken critique of such categorizations might help me in the future to visualize differences among the social workers without losing track of other analytical discussions. Such a context could therefore give me a possibility to develop more profoundly on differences between the social workers, and possible motivations to act based on, for example, their own experiences of migration.

Notes

1 According to the Dublin II Regulation, every person seeking refuge should do so by filing an application in the first country of arrival. This means that Sweden at this time (in 2012) was deporting minors to other EU countries placed at the EU borders, such as Malta, Italy and Hungary.

2 All quotes from social workers are also presented in my PhD thesis (Nordling 2017) and are translated from Swedish by me.

3 The empirical material discussed in this chapter draws on 14 interviews performed between 2011 and 2014 with social assistants (working to provide housing and schooling etc. to unaccompanied minors), personnel at accommodation centres (working closely with the everyday life of the minors) and guardians (who should see to the minors' interests and can make decisions concerning personal, legal and economic issues).

4 During my time as a PhD student I was situated between the fields of social work and critical border and migration studies. Within the field of social work, where I was situated academically, there was on the one hand a critique of social work practice as disciplinary, and on the other hand there was a tradition of seeing social workers as agents who work in support of service users. Within the field of critical migration studies, where I felt at home as a researcher, I often encountered an image of social workers as being a part of the deportation machinery; agents who – although maybe with good intentions – were

upholding the exclusionary welfare state bureaucracy. I could see that all these views had relevancy, and this fact created dilemmas in my writing.

5 For a discussion on ambivalence within Swedish No Border activism, see Söderman (2019).
6 For an overview of such critiques, see Sager *et al.* (2016).
7 For example, using fictive characters or vignettes could have been a way to contextualize the positions of the individual social workers, and make their acts more understandable.
8 The Sweden Democrats are a nationalist, far-right party.

References

Aracena, P., 2015. Rasismen inom välfärdens ramar [Racism within the framework of welfare]. In: A. Groglopo, M. Allelin, D. Mulinari and C. Días, eds. *Vardagens antirasism. Om rörelsens villkor och framväxt i Sverige [Everyday antiracism. On the conditions and growth of it in Sweden]*. Stockholm: Antirastistiska akademin.

Back, L., 2007. *The art of listening*. Oxford: Berg.

Balibar, É., 2004. *We, the people of Europe?* Princeton; Oxford: Princeton University Press.

Dant, T., 2003. *Critical social theory: Culture, society & critique*. London: SAGE.

Fassin, D., 2007. Humanitarianism as a politics of life. *Public Culture*, 19 (3), 499–520.

Fassin, D., 2015. Conclusion: Raisons d'état. In: D. Fassin et al., eds. *At the heart of the state. The moral world of institutions*. London: Pluto Press.

Ferguson, I., 2007. *Reclaiming social work: Challenging neo-liberalism and promoting social justice*. London: SAGE.

Gruber, S., 2016. Cultural competence in institutional care for youths: Experts with ambivalent positions. *Nordic Journal of Social Research*, 1 (13), 89–101.

Hammar, T., 1999. Closing the doors to the Swedish welfare state. In: G. Brochman and T. Hammar, eds. *Mechanisms of migration control: A comparative analysis of European regulation policies*. Oxford: Berg.

Hedin, U.-C., Månsson, S.-A. and Tikkanen, R., 2009. *När man måste säga ifrån: Om kritik och whistleblowing i offentliga organisationer [When to speak: About criticism and whistleblowing in public organizations]*. Stockholm: Natur och kultur.

Hemmings, C., 2018. A feminist politics of ambivalence: Reading with Emma Goldman. *Estudos Feministas*, 26 (3), 1–11.

Hermansson, L. et al., 2020. Firewalls: A necessary tool to enable social rights for undocumented migrants in social work. *International Social Work*. doi:10.1177/0020872820924454.

Isin, E, 2008. Theorizing acts of citizenship. In: E. Isin and G. Nielsen, eds. *Acts of citizenship*. London: Zed Books.

Isin, E., 2012. *Citizens without frontiers*. New York: Bloomsbury.

Kamali, M., 2015. *War, Violence and Social Justice*. Farnham: Ashgate.

Khondker, H.H. and Schuerkens, U., 2014. Social transformation, development and globalization. *Sociopedia.isa*. doi:10.1177/205684601423

Lauri, M., 2016. *Narratives of governing: Rationalization, responsibility and resistance in social work*. Thesis (PhD). Umeå University.

Lister, R., 2009. A Nordic nirvana? Gender, citizenship, and social justice in the Nordic welfare states. *Social Politics: International Studies in Gender, State and Society*, 16 (2), 242–278.

Maestri, G. and Monforte, P., 2020. Who deserves compassion? The moral and emotional dilemmas of volunteering in the 'refugee crisis'. *Sociology*, 54 (5), 1–16.

Magnusson, E., 2016. *Löfvén: Striderna i Mosul talar för fortsatta gränskontroller [Löfvén: The fighting in Mosul calls for continued border controls]*. 17 October 2016 Available from: https://

www.sydsvenskan.se/2016-10-17/lofven-striderna-i-mosul-talar-for-fortsatta-granskon-troller/[Accessed 26 August 2020].

Martinsson, L., Griffin, G. and Nygren, K.G., eds. 2016. *Challenging the myth of gender equality in Sweden*. Bristol: Policy Press.

Martinsson, L. and Mulinari, D., eds. 2018. *Dreaming global change, Doing local feminisms. Visions of feminism. Global North/Global South encounters, conversations and disagreements*. London: Routledge.

Martinsson, L. and Reimers, E., 2020. Civil servants talk back: Political subjectivity and (re) construction of the nation. *Critical Sociology*, 46 (3), 429–442.

McNevin, A., 2012. Undocumented citizens? Shifting grounds of citizenship in Los Angeles. In: P. Nyers and K. Rygiel, eds. *Citizenship, migrant activism and the politics of movement*. New York: Routledge.

NBTV, 2015. *Goda exempel i socialtjänsten – på riktigt [Good examples in the social services – for real]*. Available from: https://nbvt.wordpress.com/goda-exempel-i-socialtjansten-pa-riktigt/ [Accessed 2 December 2015].

Nielsen, A., 2016. *Challenging rightlessness: On irregular migrants and the contestation of welfare state demarcation in Sweden*. Thesis (PhD). Linnaeus University.

Nordling, V., 2017. *Destabilising citizenship practices? Social work and undocumented migrants in Sweden*. Thesis (PhD). Lund University.

Nordling, V., Sager, M. and Söderman, E., 2017. From citizenship to mobile commons: Reflections on the local struggles of undocumented migrants in the city of Malmö, Sweden. *Citizenship Studies*, 21 (6), 710–726.

Nordling, V., Klöfvermark, J. and Sigvardsdotter, E., 2020 forthcoming. *Föräldraskap efter flykt till ett annat land [Parenting after fleeing to another country]*. Report. The Swedish Red Cross University College.

Nyers, P., 2008. No one is illegal between city and Nation. In: E. Isin and G. Nielsen, eds. *Acts of citizenship*. London: Zed Books.

Panican, A. and Ulmestig, R., 2016. Social rights in the shadow of poor relief: Social assistance in the universal Swedish welfare state. *Citizenship Studies*, 20 (3–4), 475–489.

Persdotter, M. and Nordling, V., 2020 forthcoming. Bordering through destitution: The case of social assistance to irregularised migrants in Malmö, Sweden. Draft submitted for *Nordic Social Work Research*, special issue on 'Border policing in the social service sector'.

Picozza, F., 2017. *Producing Europe's geographies of asylum: Ethnographic reflections on helping, solidarity and self-organisation in Hamburg during and after the 'refugee crisis'*. Seminar 25 October 2017, SOAS University of London. Available from: https://www.soas.ac.uk/migrationdiaspora/seminarsevents/seminarseries/25oct2017-producing-europes-geographies-of-asylum-ethnographic-reflections-on-helping-solidarity-and.html [Accessed 20 June 2020].

Pickering, L. and Kara, H., 2017. Presenting and representing others: Towards an ethics of engagement. *International Journal of Social Research Methodology*. doi:10.1080/13645579.2 017.1287875

Regeringskansliet, 2015. *Tal av Stefan Löfvén vid manifestationen för flyktingar den 5 september [Speech by Stefan Löfvén at the demonstration for refugees on 5 September]*. 2015-09-05 Available from: https://www.regeringen.se/tal/2015/09/tal-av-stefan-lofven-vid-manifestationen-for-flyktingar-den-5-september/ [Accessed 11 August 2020].

Sager, M., 2011. *Everyday clandestinity. Experiences on the margins of citizenship and migration policies*. Thesis (PhD). Lund University.

Sager, M., 2015. Förändringar och tystnader, utopier och kompromisser – En reflektion över kampen för migranters rättigheter [Changes and silences, utopias and compromises: A reflection on the fight for migrants' rights]. In: A. Groglopo, M. Allelin, D. Mulinari and C. Días, eds. *Vardagens Antirasism. Om rörelsens villkor och framväxt i Sverige [Everyday antiracism. On the conditions and growth of it in Sweden]*. Stockholm: Antirastistiska akademin.

Sager, M., Holgersson, H. and Öberg, K., eds. 2016. *Irreguljär Migration i Sverige. Rättigheter, vardagserfarenheter, motstånd och statliga kategoriseringar [Irregular migration in Sweden. Rights, everyday experiences, resistance and government categorizations]*. Göteborg: Daidalos.

Sandusky, L., 2017. Dust of the desert. In: C. Milstein, ed. *Rebellious mourning*, Chico: AK Press.

Schierup, C.-U. and Ålund, A., 2011. The end of Swedish exceptionalism? Citizenship, neoliberalism and the politics of exclusion. *Race & Class*, 53 (1), 45–64.

Söderman, E., 2019. *Resistance through acting: Ambivalent practices of the No Border Musical*. Thesis (PhD). Lund University.

Ticktin, M., 2011. *Casualties of care: Immigration and the politics of humanitarianism in France*. Berkeley: University of California Press.

Whitson, R., 2017. Painting pictures of ourselves. Researcher subjectivity in the practice of feminist reflexivity. *The Professional Geographer*, 69 (2), 299–306.

Wikström, H., 2013. Ett postkolonialt perspektiv på sociala problem [A postcolonial perspective on social problems]. In: A. Meeuwisse et al., eds. *Perspektiv på sociala problem [Perspective on social problems]*. Stockholm: Natur & Kultur.

vistårinteut (2019) *Öppet brev till socialdemokraterna [Open letter to the Social Democrats]*. 23 March 2019. Available from: https://vistarinteut.org/oppet-brev-till-socialdemokraterna/ [Accessed 3 September 2020].

7
THE ETHICS OF RENAMING

On challenges and dilemmas of anonymization in a study of anti-Muslim racism

Marta Kolankiewicz

Anonymization is a standard procedure in social scientific research today. However, while formal ethical codes, including the requirement to protect participants' privacy, are more and more broadly applied, some doubts about the feasibility and implications of anonymization have been voiced. Ethnographers and other researchers using qualitative methods have questioned whether it is in general possible to render their research participants fully anonymous (see, e.g., Nespor 2000, van den Hoonaard 2003). It has also been questioned as to what extent anonymization is desirable, or even ethical, in the context of participatory research (e.g., Walford 2005, Berkhout 2013). Finally, the impact of anonymization on data and on the analysis itself has been discussed (Vainio 2012).

This chapter engages with the issue of anonymization[1] by exploring different relations between anonymization, empirical material, analysis, theorization and ethics. It focuses on the ways in which anonymization procedures in research on the topic of racism are intrinsically intertwined with the analytical and theoretical work. In my discussion, I draw on the experience of anonymization in a study of Swedish court cases addressing anti-Muslim violence that bear the hallmarks of racism (Kolankiewicz 2015, 2019). In practice, anonymization most frequently comes down to erasing or changing the names of the researched persons and other details in the material that might lead to identifying those involved in the research. But what does it mean to remove a name or to rename a person in the context of research on racism? What sort of practical procedure does it require and what dilemmas does such a procedure open up for? How does this practice change the material? What influence does it have on the analysis? What kinds of ethical challenges can this practice involve? And when and why, although performed for the sake of ethics, can renaming the researched participants *feel* unethical?

The study and situating the practice of anonymization in different disciplinary traditions

The idea of the study, first written as a PhD thesis, 'Anti-Muslim Violence and the Possibility of Justice', and then published as a book, *Anti-Muslim Racism on Trial*, was to explore what happens in Swedish courts with cases that might involve anti-Muslim racism. As in many other countries in Europe, the Swedish legal system is equipped with tools to fight different expressions of racism. These range from the prohibition of agitation against a national or ethnic group, through anti-discrimination legislation, to the penalty-enhancement provision for crimes motivated by racism. The aims of the study were to see how these legal tools work in practice and in particular with regard to anti-Muslim racism, to analyze their potential and their limitations, and thus, more generally, to explore the possibility of reaching justice in court in cases involving racism. I was interested in the ways in which the judiciary deals with such crimes, and also I wanted to see whether and how the possible racist hallmarks of the acts on trial are described, defined and taken into consideration in judgements. To achieve these aims, I looked at the ways in which courts adjudicate when handling concrete cases. My choice was to access such cases through Brå, the Swedish National Board for Crime Prevention, which is a national body responsible for collecting statistics on, among other things, hate crime in Sweden. Brå is independent of the judiciary and has developed quite a sophisticated system for identifying cases of hate crimes. From them, I received the material on Islamophobic hate crimes drawn from a period of four years: both statistical and textual data consisting of crime descriptions from police reports of around 1,000 cases. The second step for me was to follow about 50 cases that went to court and collect complete police and court documents concerning the selected cases. These became the material for my study.

I had started thinking about the anonymization when applying for approval of my project from the Board of Ethics. The Board is governed by different legal regulations and the requirements and definitions provided by the Swedish Research Council, where one of the main rules is of confidentiality. The procedures of protecting personal data might often seem mechanical, focusing on the practicalities of keeping the material safe and technicalities of detaching the data from the identities of particular individuals. The language of the ethical codes and regulations bears clear reference to the field of medicine, disclosing the genealogy of the official academic ethical codes. Still, the codes give the impression of universality and unanimity across different disciplines regarding anonymization procedures.

However, protecting identities of those involved in research is not a purely formal obligation. Anonymization is an established practice and a default position in sociology that stems from a preoccupation with the protection of the identity of those researched. It is grounded in a long tradition of a critique of science, including social sciences, as running the risk of treating those studied in an objectifying way and exposing them to harm. It is also an expression of the awareness of the power of knowledge produced at universities. The practice of anonymization has deeply influenced the way in which material collected through qualitative interviews and ethnographic fieldwork has been conventionally presented in sociological writing. From the very beginning, therefore, my approach to anonymization was grounded in two fields: the legal regulations concerning the treatment of personal data, on the one hand, and the sociological tradition, on the other.

At the same time, by focusing on the judiciary and its interpretation of the law in my project, I was also entering the field of legal scholarly tradition. In this context, it is important to mention that various documents produced by courts and police have different statuses in Sweden. Court decisions (*dom*) are public documents, which means that they are accessible to everybody. The status of the preliminary enquiry reports (*förundersökningsprotokoll*) produced by the police depends on what happens with cases. These documents become public once the prosecutor has pressed charges, which applied to all the police documents I wanted to focus on in my study. However, even then, they often contain sensitive personal data that might be confidential, in which cases the authority in question considers whether or not to grant access to a document or part thereof. The principle of public access to official records (*offentlighetsprincipen*) is very strong in Sweden. Not only is case law from the Supreme Court published, but anybody can request any court decision unless it is confidential. Moreover, those requesting the documents do not need to provide any particular reason for doing so and can even remain anonymous themselves. This principle is one of the cornerstones of the Swedish legal system set up not only to encourage free exchange of opinions in the democratic society, but also to guarantee the rule of law and transparency through citizens' insight into the working of the judiciary and trials (Bohlin 2015, pp. 19–20). It is partly due to this tradition that anonymization is not treated in absolute terms by legal scholars. The precedents from the Swedish Supreme Court and from the Courts of Appeal are published in the *New Archive of Law* (*Nytt juridiskt arkiv*). Conventionally, the names of the parties are replaced by their initials in these publications, but the case numbers are given, so that it is always possible to track the cases and identify those involved in them. In legal scholarship, it is not only a custom to provide case numbers of the analyzed cases, but it is understood as a good practice and way of enabling other scholars to verify the accuracy and validity of the analysis (for how this practice is changing in Sweden in light of new laws on personal data protection, see Persson 2019). It is thus a question of the transparency of research – itself a crucial ethical issue. While I was cognizant of this tradition, it was only at the end of my research – when a judge whom I asked to read and comment on my text showed surprise that I had not provided the case numbers – that I understood the centrality of the issue of transparency and the ethical implications that it had in the field of legal scholarship.

By working at the intersection of these disciplines, I became aware of different readings and traditions of the ethical codes and of the diverse tensions in their application. The rigid rules of ethics formulated in an absolute and universal way in the codes turned out to be much more disputed and ambivalent when used in practice in different disciplines. However, it was only in the practical work with anonymization that I fully grasped the complexity of the ethics of renaming the people involved in the research.

Erasing names

The first step in the anonymization procedure was to eliminate proper names from the documents. I removed not only the names of individuals, but also places, dates and other details, and for that, I used a system in which the erased words were substituted by 'NAME', 'DATE', 'PLACE' and so on. At this point, the anonymization was done directly in the material; the procedure was aimed at making it safe to work on it. While this procedure helped me to work on a large amount of documents without their containing any personal data, it entailed some problems. I soon realized that some components of the material had become difficult to differentiate: many people who were in one way or another involved in the cases had blended together.

This realization occurred in parallel with a new phase in my work on the material. By now, I was occupied mostly by the cases that went to court and reading the judgements. At this stage, my analytical work involved ordering the material, by dividing it into different categories. I was interested in discovering *patterns* in the judiciary's way of treating the acts on trial, which led to creating a database of all the cases that went to the court. I used the database as a way of performing a kind of descriptive statistics of the cases, which would show the diverse ways in which the court could approach the possible racist character of the acts on trial. These ranged from the application of the penalty enhancement because of racist motives and an explicit reference to the racist dimension of the crime in the judgement, through a lack of any reference to this dimension in the acts on trial, to the rejection of the possibility that the acts might involve racism. In addition to this more quantitative work, I wanted to extract and use the quotes from the court documents to illustrate these different ways of approaching the possibility of a racist character of the acts on trial. I realized that it was difficult to work on the textual data as anonymized in the way described above. What I needed was to be able to clearly and easily distinguish between the roles that different people had in a trial: those of the injured party, the defendant and witnesses.

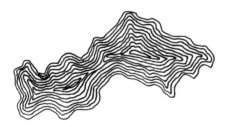

In order to make the material more intelligible, I decided to introduce codes for these different roles. Thus, I coded the names of the defendants as XX, the injured parties as YY, witnesses as WW, names of locations as PP, case numbers as

NN, dates as DD, ethnicity of a person or a group as EE, etc. I will illustrate how this kind of anonymization could work with a quote from a paper that I presented to a conference at that time. The anonymized quotes from court documents are here integrated into the analysis, and I think it is interesting to see how analysis and anonymization work together to create a certain effect.

Struggling for a definition, pronouncing ambiguous sentences

Two cases may illustrate the struggle to define and interpret an act as racist or not which took place in court. Each case was considered by two courts: first by a District Court and then by a Court of Appeal, with opposite results.

In Case 25 a man was accused of unlawful threat, molestation and insult. He had been calling by phone his ex-wife both at home and at work. On one occasion, he insulted and threatened her colleague, using expressions like: 'fucking Arab', 'Muslim idiot', 'wife-beater' and 'you little Arab fag'. The District Court found him guilty of molestation and insult and argued:

'Although there were accusations from both sides and although there was only brief mention of YY's race and religion, the acts must be regarded as molestation and insult and the crimes shall have increased penal value.' (Case 25, District Court)

An appeal was lodged and the Court of Appeal overruled this decision. The Court of Appeal referred to the above-mentioned legislative history in the discussion about whether a 'racist motive' or 'racist feature' of a crime took place. The court noticed that on that occasion it was decided that the provision should apply only to crimes with a racist motive and concluded:

'In the light of the foregoing and considering that nothing has shown that XX's motive with the acts was to offend YY because of race or the like, there is no reason to apply the aforementioned penalty-enhancement provision.'

(Case 25, Court of Appeal)

Scholars have discussed the question of what ontological implications and analytical functions the procedure of anonymization may have. Vainio, for example, claims that anonymization entails converting text into data. In this sense, anonymization is not innocent in regard to the empirical material; it actually leads to an important change in it (Vainio 2012, pp. 4–5). Something happens in the process, in which parts of material that had to do with the singularity of the stories, realities and worlds that the data concerns get lost. This has significant implications for the analytical process. In a way, anonymization has become, particularly in the sociological tradition, one of the tools for theorization and generalization. In some styles of sociological ethnography and interview studies, research participants are turned into a collection of people to 'represent presupposed theoretical categories' (Nespor 2000, p. 550). One of the most famous representatives of such a genre would be Goffman, whose accounts on asylum or stigma, for instance, create examples of places and people that are located in a kind of abstract everywhere/nowhere space. In this tradition, particular stories become unanchored and sectioned off from the ongoing practices to become 'descriptive fragments illustrating constructs of sociological discourse' or 'floating theoretical exemplars' (Nespor 2000, pp. 552–553).

This is what I was actually doing with my analysis. While I believed that the new anonymization technique made it easier to comprehend the analyzed texts as accounts of an interaction between the parties in court, it also shaped my material in a significant way. After my initial reading of the material, my main finding was that anti-Muslim racism had in the vast majority of cases not been attended to in court. The acts on trial would often be named, classified and judged as different types of crime, but the racist dimension was rarely addressed in the judgement. It was often not even considered. In this way, racism was made invisible in the judicial process. My aim, at this stage, was to document and classify this process. The statistics of different ways in which racism could be approached in court which I compiled served as the main instrument to do this. The sections of my textual material – quotes from police files and court documents – were to illustrate these statistics. In this sense, particular individuals were reduced to their role in the trial and their stories were used by me to prove my point. The particularities were irrelevant to the major argument. My task became to present evidence that would support my argument. As I have analyzed elsewhere (Kolankiewicz 2015, 2019), my reliance on the quantitative method was connected to a particular force and persuasiveness of the tradition of knowledge production that relies on statistical thinking. It also ran parallel to the methods used by the courts themselves to establish truth and produce knowledge about the events they judge.

> In reaction to a silence around the type of injury caused by anti-Muslim racism that I discovered in the documents I was studying, I found myself eager to prove the existence of this kind of injury and of its unrecognition by the courts. […] I started to use the epistemological approach and methodological tools of the judiciary in order to produce a reliable account. My early attempts to analyze and present the material in a quantitative way were shaped by the ideal endorsed by the judiciary of what incontrovertible evidence is and how truth can be established and fixed.
>
> (Kolankiewicz 2019, p. 37)

My anonymization technique seemed to be in line with this analytical strategy. By fusing different people involved in the trials into their roles as the defendants, injured parties, and witnesses, the particular cases were remodelled as instances of the patterns of courts' unrecognition. The specificities and context became irrelevant to my main findings and argument to be proved.

Renaming

After some time of analytical work, my strategies considerably shifted, and this shift also involved an important change in the anonymization technique. Principally, it entailed abandoning the quantitative frames. I concluded that there were limits to the analytical strategy when accumulating and mixing quotes detached from their cases in order to instantiate a particular typology or classification. There were several reasons for this. As mentioned above, I was becoming aware of the ways in which I was imitating the judiciary and its methods of presenting reliable evidence. I was also trying to overcome a kind of anxiety that had to do with being able to attend to the particularities and singularities of the stories of violence that I was confronted with in my material. To treat the cases as statistics – numbers and dry illustrations detached from the real lives of people – felt somehow strange. And I slowly came to realize that one of the reasons for this was that the judicial language in which the courts describe the cases and express their judgements was dry and distanced in a somewhat similar way. Giving names to the people whose stories came to me through the court documents was a way of rehumanizing them. It was also a way for me to find a writing style and language in which I wanted to speak, and this was done *in relation* to the language of the court documents.

This new writing style consisted in focusing on a selected few cases that I narrated in a more ethnographic style. The cases were to help me to understand the rationale behind the court judgements and in particular, the reasons for the peculiar silence around the possible racist character of the acts on trial. From the work of ethnographers, I learned how a thick description of singular instances of the studied forms of social life can open up for an interpretation that attends to the dynamics of these forms in their particularity (Sheldon 2016). Thus, my ambition was to capture, or more exactly to reconstruct, from the court documents particularities of the stories of different trials and of the acts addressed in court. I was in a way experimenting in doing an ethnography through an archive, being inspired, on the one hand, by a thick description (Geertz 1973) of the ethnographic genre and, on the other, by a Foucauldian historical style of describing forms of life in the past (for instance, in Foucault 1995). I felt that this combination helped me to reinsert the cases into their context, to reattach those involved to their particular stories and to represent them more fully. The fragment below provides an example of what such a description looks like in the final version of the book.

> On a June night, on his way to morning prayer, Mustafa Al-Basri discovered that the local mosque situated in a flat in a residential block in Manby – a small village in Sweden – was burning. He called the fire brigade. The fire-fighters soon arrived and put out the fire. The room's curtains were burnt, as well as the rugs that stretched across the floor. The walls were covered with soot and the flat was filled with smoke, which had started to spread into the communal stairwell. Mustafa Al-Basri also found a Koran thrown on the ground outside the mosque. Over the following days, the police would receive several religious books that belonged to the Muslim community and had been kept in the mosque, but were now found all around the village.
>
> In the course of the investigation, it became clear that the fire had been started by somebody, and a local young man, Sven Persson, confessed that he had entered the mosque twice that night. On the first occasion, he took some

books from a bookshelf and afterwards threw them away in different places around the village while wandering the streets with a group of friends. On the second occasion, he dropped a match in the mosque. Persson was charged with theft and arson and, some months later, his trial took place.

(Kolankiewicz 2019, pp. 102–103)

Reworking the analysis and rewriting the text meant therefore using a different anonymization technique. Now I anonymized the cases according to the ethnographic convention, using pseudonyms. Turning the abstract XX and YY back into persons located in the particular histories of violence and then involved in trials was achieved partly by restoring names to them – not their own ones, though, but new, fictive ones that I found for them. This anonymization technique changed the material in a different way, and in many senses this change was even more profound. Since I was committed to protecting the identities of those involved, and since the cases were now depicted in more detail, anonymization required much more intervention: not only proper names but also certain details of the cases had to be changed in order to decrease the risk of identification.

Names and the anxiety of representation

The new anonymization procedure helped to some extent to relieve the sensation of discomfort related to the treatment of those involved in the cases I analyzed as specimens of categories used to illustrate my argument. But, while this procedure was also motivated by ethical considerations, it soon transpired to bring new problems and dilemmas.

One of the first consequences of the procedure of naming was the realization of the fact that names are not 'meaningless markers' that denote without connotation as J.S. Mill claimed (Mill 1974[1843], cited Vom Bruck and Bodenhorn 2007, p. 5). The process of anonymization – consisting in the elimination or reduction of the denotative function of proper names – made their connotative function more visible. Suddenly the names of those involved in trials became all about the connotation. And this connotation seemed to play a crucial role in the understanding of the cases I was studying. The first and most critical one turned out to be the ways in which these names were connoted with particular groups. When choosing new names, it was of crucial importance to retain some of these connotations. Thus, that a name sounded ethnically Swedish or suggested a certain immigrant background seemed to be relevant and important.

Although this procedure was applied to all those involved in the trials, apart from the members of the judiciary and law enforcement system, who were referred to as the generic 'judge', 'prosecutor' or 'police officer',[2] I will focus here on the anonymization of the injured parties – people who had been exposed to different types of acts of violence. These acts were interesting to me because they potentially had a particular character: they could be treated as acts of anti-Muslim racism. The fact that the injured parties were or could be perceived as Muslims was thus of central importance to my study. Although in none of the cases that I analyzed did the name or surname of the injured party seem to have been a direct trigger for the acts of violence or to have played a role in identifying the injured party as a Muslim, I was aware that names are considered to be one of the most important signifiers of Muslim identity in Sweden and 'a forceful device of stigmatization' (Khosravi 2012, p. 69). In some contexts, names could thus serve to identify an individual as belonging to a particular community. While I stripped the people in my study of their original names, it was still important to me to retain the possibility for a reader to identify them as potentially perceived as Muslims. This meant that I could not just pick random names; I did not even know what a random name would be. I could change individual names, but I had to keep the generic connotation that the names engendered and that indicated their belonging to a group against which the acts that my study was concerned with were directed, that is Muslims.

Even so, this practice of renaming gave me a sensation of discomfort. It was puzzling that a procedure aimed at protecting those who were involved in the cases could actually feel somehow wrong. Initially, I took this discomfort as related to a more general anxiety concerning representation that was here closely linked to the idea that naming represented a symbolic dimension of power. In a sense, to erase the original names and to substitute them with new ones, that I myself selected, meant that I was creating a new denotation for the names. The link between the names and the referents – the real people – was now broken, and the new names started now to refer to a *representation* of people involved in the cases that I was describing, a representation that I was creating – an image that resembled the original, but that was not the same as the original. And the anxiety was related to the violence that in turn is related to the ethnographic authority involved in this act of representing (cf. Hastrup 1992). Still, it dawned on me that there was something more specific to the context of my research, that is, to the study of racism.

Names and racism

Since I worked in the post-colonial tradition, I was well aware of the ways in which naming played a role in the colonial project. The history of European conquest of the Americas has been marked by the widespread practice of naming that was deeply embedded in the project of dominating and taking into possession the conquered lands. One of the most telling examples comes from the journals of Christopher Columbus that witness what Tzvetan Todorov described as Columbus's 'veritable naming frenzy': Columbus would name islands, pieces of land, water and everywhere he reached – giving new names to these places was equivalent to taking into possession (Todorov 1999, p. 27). In one of the most extreme of colonial institutions, slavery, such naming as a means of taking into possession had to do with people. Susan Benson describes the pervasive practice of renaming slaves in the context of European, Caribbean and North American chattel slavery: 'slavery embedded in a cultural and legal milieu where the significance of the "proper name" – the name one "answers to," the name that defines an individual's legal and social identity, is inextricably linked to western ideas of autonomous selfhood and of social capacity' (Benson 2007, pp. 181–182). She shows how the practice of renaming was related to a privilege of recognition that corresponded to holding power over those renamed. Moreover, she discusses how new names given to slaves – that would often become conventional slave names – were in themselves injurious, having a function of indicating an allegedly incomplete personhood of the slaves. Thus, the practice of renaming has a very gloomy history and entailed a form of symbolic violence. I was also cognizant of academia's complicity in the colonial project through its representational practices, well-described by, among others, Edward Said (Said 2003). Aware of these violent histories, I sensed the burden of the practice of representation in general, and of renaming in particular. Still, my feeling of discomfort also seemed to be related to something more specific.

Gradually, I realized that this discomfort related to what the anonymization was doing with the identities of the people I wanted to protect. In anonymization, the original name is replaced by a research pseudonym. At the same time, what kind of replacement was possible here depended on the common belonging of these names to a particular category of 'Muslim-sounding' names. The relation between the name and the pseudonym could be described as a form of interchangeability. Kathleen Blee writes about the fungibility of victims as the criterion for defining the special character of racial violence. She argues that this type of violence, in contrast to other kinds of interpersonal violence, can be identified through victims' fungibility: the possibility of a victim being classified in the group by the offender is the source of the harm (Blee 2005, p. 607). It is my recourse to this very same sort of fungibility, in which racist practices were grounded, that made the procedure of anonymization awkward and difficult. This was related to the workings of interchangeability of certain names and to the risk of reducing the identities of those carrying the names to certain group (religious or ethnic) identities.

More specifically, by looking for names that could be read as Muslim, I was also connecting to my readers in particular ways, mobilizing certain kinds of knowledge and potentially opening up certain kinds of injuries. Somehow, my own practice was mimicking those that make 'a Muhammad' of every Muslim. I knew that some names have become such a strong sign of being a Muslim that they have been described as stigmas. Khosravi, who has analyzed the reasons, expectations and effects of name-changing by Muslims in Sweden, writes about this kind of stigma as one of the main causes behind name-changing in this group of people. One of the names that is most frequently dropped is 'Muhammad', which in the context of various 'Muhammad cartoon affairs' 'has become a name to designate a person who is not socially and culturally connected to Swedishness. [...] Muslims are turned into *a* Muhammad. Like the Cohen regularly featured in anti-Semitic jokes and songs, the name Muhammad also often figures in jokes about Muslims' (Khosravi 2012, p. 70). Khosravi writes that this type of stigmatization of names implicates the invisibility as an individual as opposed to visibility as a type, that is, as a member of a particular minority (Khosravi 2012, p. 73). And this was what the procedure of anonymization was actually doing: its aim was to make individual people involved in trials unrecognizable as individuals; to make them invisible was the main strategy of providing them anonymity or protecting their identities. At the same time, in this process, the characteristics of the proper names that could make it possible to identify the individuals as part of a certain group were kept, making the persons visible as a type.

But there was yet another dimension to this. Since I chose to carry out an in-depth analysis of a few case studies, the risk of disclosing the identities of those involved was greater than in previous analytical strategies. It became even more imperative to conceal or change details that could lead to identification in the cases. One of the ways to go in such situations is to make more invasive changes that would devoid the case of several particularities. What I decided for my study had to do with the ethnic connotation of the names. So, while keeping the Muslim-sounding names, I would switch among ethnic groups; this was feasible considering the fact that Swedish Muslims are one of the most diverse and heterogeneous Muslim populations in Europe. This diversity stems partly from different migratory histories: from Turkish labour immigration in the 1970s, through Kurds, Iranians and Palestinians fleeing war and conflict, as well as refugees from Somalia and Ethiopia in the 1980s, to large groups of Muslims from the Balkan states in the 1990s (Larsson 2009, Sander 2004), and to Iraqis, Syrians and Afghanis in the most recent years. I could thus change the ethnicity by choosing from among a large variety of Swedish Muslim communities, thereby diminishing the risk of the cases being linked to the original groups. By the same token, this procedure relied on a treatment of Muslims *en bloc*: as members of one large group, again risking reproducing the very Islamophobia often characterized as grounded in a view of Islam as a homogeneous bloc (as defined in the now classic report, *Islamophobia: A Challenge for Us All*, 1997).

Moreover, in this procedure, some important aspects of these different instances of violence were being lost or erased. Particular histories of marginalization, discrimination and oppression were being obliterated. This was in turn somehow impacting on the analysis and my understanding of anti-Muslim racism. These particularities could be equally important for understanding today's anti-Muslim racisms in Sweden as the common experience of being targeted as a Muslim. By making these differences of the experiences visible, I could have told the story of anti-Muslim racism as a multifaceted phenomenon deeply embedded in the distinct histories of diverse groups in which particular genealogies and histories played an important part in how racism would be articulated. Different groups had disparate relations to the history of colonialization and migratory paths; diverse ethnicities and skin colours occupied distinct places in the racist imaginary; and these differences could also be visible in ways of relating to the Islamic religion itself. Thus, understanding the *particularities* of distinct collective histories of oppression across Muslim communities in Sweden was significant for the understanding of specific articulations of anti-Muslim racism. And making the belonging to particular ethnic groups exchangeable resulted in concealing one scale of anti-Muslim racism and had an influence on my analysis of the phenomenon. Moreover, and maybe ethically more significant, this was also a question of the *singularities* of the stories that I was analyzing, since belonging to certain groups could also be formative in the subjectivities of the people whom I was naming and representing.

This type of problem was insightfully described by Shahram Khosravi, who, in his auto-ethnography, recalls and analyzes how his experience of being shot by the 'Laser Man'[3] became a public issue and what it meant to be 'renamed, re-shaped and re-defined' (Khosravi 2010, p. 82). He describes how the representation of himself and his story felt violent and how it was often distorted in media and books. One of the instances of such a distortion had to do with the anonymization: 'To make it even worse, I was renamed "Ali". Under the photo it read: "Ali thanks God he survived." I was called Ali (a name with more Islamic connotations than Shahram) and was presented as a religious person' (Khosravi 2010, p. 83). It is difficult to tell whether in the case described by Khosravi the distortion had to do with deliberate manipulation or rather with ignorance. In any case, the result was a kind of misrepresentation. So, while the risk of mimicking racist practices when anonymizing had to do with shameful cultural literacy in names' significance and connotations, the risk of distortion could stem, on the contrary, from a kind of cultural illiteracy. These seemed to be two sides of the same coin, showing a particular place in the connotative field of Muslim names in Sweden, and more generally in the West. A study of racism bore a danger of reducing the racialized individuals and their stories to their experience of racism, and this reduction had begun already with the naming.

But the discomfort that I was experiencing in the process of renaming those whose stories I was analyzing might have to do with yet another thing. Calling the participants by proper names forced me to engage with the singularity of their stories, and these were filled with scenes of violence. In this way, the process represented also an ethical commitment to, and suggested boundaries of, the possibility of relating to the suffering of the other.[4] The process of anonymization was thus also about how different analytical strategies, those focusing on the general and those keeping the focus on the singular, open up the questions: How can we relate to the violence that is done to the other? What are the ethics of such engagement?[5]

Speaking in one's own name

It has been questioned and criticized as to whether anonymization is indeed the best tool for an ethical representation of those involved in research. Feminist and other scholars practising participatory research concerned with the issues of empowerment of marginalized groups have been advocating the possibility of research participants to *speak in their own name*. Parallel to this, within the tradition of oral histories, researchers have criticized the practice of anonymization for being in contradiction to the project of 'giving voice' that this type of research aimed at. In some projects, to make it possible to speak in one's own name meant making visible those who in the social realities are pushed to the margins and are devoid of any power, including over one's own representation (cf. e.g., Back 2007). In other contexts, anonymity has been questioned by research participants themselves speaking from the position of political subjects shaped 'by ethical experiences of dispossession, interconnectedness and vulnerability'. In such contexts, speaking in one's own name can be vital, because in order to be political 'we must somehow commit to the particularity of our own experience as the ground for staking a more general claim' (Sheldon 2016, pp. 164–165).

While these more abstract political and ethical issues point to the crucial intersection between knowledge production and the issues of representation and recognition, they resonated in the material collected in my project in a very specific way. As mentioned, I accessed both the accounts of the trial and the accounts of the actual acts on trial exclusively through court and police documents. This meant that the testimonies of these experiences came to me narrated in the third person and mediated through the authoritative account of the judiciary (Kolankiewicz 2015, p. 127). In a sense, the workings of the legal language are here at their most visible – framing the accounts of the experiences of those involved. By using the grammatical construction of indirect speech, the court *is speaking in their name*. My concern in regard to this was that my representation, although trying to reclaim the voices of those involved in the trials, was actually also a way of speaking in their name. This revealed the limits of the knowledge produced in academia and its similarities to the one produced in court: I was still speaking in their name.

Notes

1 I understand anonymization here as a procedure aimed at protecting the privacy of those researched by removing, covering or obscuring identifiers from the data. In parts of the literature a distinction is made between the terms 'anonymization' and 'de-identification': while the former means to irreversibly break all the links between the material and a concrete person, the latter means a process by which the links are broken but it could be possible to re-identify the research participants, e.g. through a confidential key produced in the process. In practice, most of the time, researchers de-identify the participants; nevertheless, I use the concept of anonymization since it has become a more general term to designate the procedures aimed at guaranteeing the confidentiality of the research participants or protecting their privacy.

2 The decision to keep these generic styles of referring to those representing the judiciary was also related to a particular way of treating the judiciary as a system and not approaching those who act as a part of the system as situated individuals with belonging to a specific class or to an ethnic or religious group. In one sense, this decision was consistent with how the judiciary represents itself – as a neutral and independent system in which all the decisions are made in a way that respects an individual's right to a fair trial and grounded only in the law independent of who is actually exercising judgement. Giving names to judges would have made them visible as situated subjects and not just cogs in the machine. It could also disclose particular structural problems that the Swedish judiciary faces, in terms of power relations and lack of representation of large segments of society.

3 A serial killer who shot several people with immigrant background in Stockholm and Uppsala in the 1990s.

4 I am grateful to Ruth Sheldon for making me pay attention to the distinction between particularities and singularities in this context and for helping me to understand my own anxiety when engaging with the *singularities* of the stories I was analyzing.

5 In asking these questions, I am inspired by the work of Ruth Sheldon (2016). I have also learned from Veena Das's discussion on what it means for anthropological knowledge to be responsive to suffering (2007, pp. 205–221).

References

Back, L., 2007. *The art of listening*. Oxford; New York: Berg.

Benson, S., 2007. Injurious names: Naming, disavowal, and recuperation in contexts of slavery and emancipation. In: G. Vom Bruck and B. Bodenhorn, eds. *An Anthropology of Names and Naming*. Cambridge: Cambridge University Press, 178–199.

Berkhout, S.G., 2013. Private talk: Testimony, evidence, and the practice of anonymization in research. *IJFAB: International Journal of Feminist Approaches to Bioethics*, (1). 19. doi:10.2979/intjfemappbio.6.1.19.

Blee, K.M., 2005. Racial violence in the United States. *Ethnic & Racial Studies*, 28 (4), 599–619. doi:10.1080/01419870500092423.

Bohlin, A., 2015. *Offentlighetsprincipen [The principle of openness]*. Stockholm: Norstedts juridik.

Das, V., 2007. *Life and words: Violence and the descent into the ordinary*. Berkeley: University of California Press.

Foucault, M., 1995. *Discipline and punish*. New York: Vintage Books.

Geertz, C., 1973. *The interpretation of cultures*. New York: Basic Books.

Hastrup, K., 1992. Out of anthropology: The anthropologist as an object of dramatic representation. *Cultural Anthropology*, 7 (3), 327–345.

Islamophobia: A challenge for us all, 1997. Available from: https://www.runnymedetrust.org/companies/17/74/Islamophobia-A-Challenge-for-Us-All.html/.

Khosravi, S., 2010. *'Illegal' Traveller: An auto-ethnography of borders*. New York: Springer eBooks.

Khosravi, S., 2012. White masks/Muslim names: Name changes among Muslim immigrants in Sweden. *Race & Class*, 53 (3), 65–80. doi:10.1177/0306396811425986.

Kolankiewicz, M., 2015. *Anti-Muslim violence and the possibility of justice*. Thesis (PhD). Lund University.

Kolankiewicz, M., 2019. *Anti-Muslim Racism on Trial: Muslims, the Swedish judiciary and the possibility of justice*. London: Routledge.

Larsson, G., 2009. Sweden. In: G. Larsson, ed. *Islam in the Nordic and Baltic Countries*. London: Routledge, 56–75.

Nespor, J., 2000. Anonymity and place in qualitative inquiry. *Qualitative Inquiry*, 6 (4), 546–569. doi:10.1177/107780040000600408.

Persson, V., 2019. Etikprövning av rättsvetenskap [Ethical review of jurisprudence]. In: R. Arvidsson et al., eds. *Festskrift till [Party letter to] Wiweka Warnling Conradsson*. Lund: Jure, 317–332.

Said, E.W., 2003. *Orientalism*. London: Penguin.

Sander, Å., 2004. Muslims in Sweden. In: J.B.A.S.M. Anwar, ed. *State policies towards Muslim minorities: Sweden, Great Britain and Germany*. Berlin: Edition Parabolis, 203–363.

Sheldon, R., 2016. *Tragic encounters and ordinary ethics: Palestine-Israel in British universities*. Manchester: Manchester University Press.

Todorov, T., 1999. *The conquest of America: The question of the other*. 1st ed. New York: University of Oklahoma Press.

Vainio, A., 2012. Beyond research ethics: Anonymity as 'ontology', 'analysis' and 'independence'. *Qualitative Research*, 13 (6), 685–698.

van den Hoonaard, W., 2003. Is anonymity an artifact in ethnographic research? *Journal of Academic Ethics*, 1 (2), 141.

Vom Bruck, G. and Bodenhorn, B., 2007. "Entangled in histories": An introduction to the anthropology of names and naming. In: G. Vom Bruck and B. Bodenhorn, eds. *An Anthropology of Names and Naming*. Cambridge: Cambridge University Press, 1–30.

Walford, G., 2005. Research ethical guidelines and anonymity. *International Journal of Research and Method in Education*, 28 (1), 83–93.

8

CARING ENCOUNTERS IN ETHNOGRAPHIC RESEARCH

Unlearning distance and learning sharing

Eda Hatice Farsakoglu and Pouran Djampour

Emergence of this text

In this chapter, we as authors enter into a dialogue in an attempt to (re)visit caring encounters in ethnographic research.[1] The dialogue is built on our PhD research projects which we conducted with different groups of people with experiences of migration and seeking asylum in two different migratory settings. Eda's dissertation project seeks to explore the everyday and migratory experiences of Iranian queer migrants who apply for refugee status and wait for resettlement in Turkey.[2] For this study, Eda conducted multisited ethnographic fieldwork that spread between the period December 2011 and February 2014, followed by some informal/unstructured, sporadic, online research interactions. Djampour's PhD research, *Borders Crossing Bodies: The stories of eight youth with experience of migrating* (2018), retells the stories of borders through time, hope, love, dreams and resistance in the lives of young people who have migrated to Sweden. The study was conducted through ethnographic fieldwork between 2013 and 2015 in three cities in Sweden together with young participants who were in their early adulthood.

Similar to the dialogic writing of Lundberg and Farahani (2017), our text emanated from different forms and layers of co-working. Since 2015, we have been sharing moments of un/learning as a part of our engagement in the Collective (see the Preface and Introduction in this volume). We have also long been in dialogue, reading and reflecting on each other's works in progress, ideas and academic anxieties. Those moments and exchanges necessarily shaped the background of this text. Our dialogue and, thus, the text have also navigated through our research experiences, fieldwork notes and memories, as well as our personal experiences of care, caring, illness, borders and migration. Finding commonalities while acknowledging differences in our experiences and subjectivities has been crucial in doing justice to our collective work. We write from our own perspectives as well as from a position of 'us', alternating and mixing the two at times but with awareness of our multiple and shifting positionings. This kind of writing, as Lundberg and Farahani aptly put it, makes it easier to practise the basics of academic writing: 'knowledge production in dialogue with other voices, expressions and previous research' (2017, p. 80, our translation).

The work process for this chapter has also undergone varied forms of collaboration. We began by exchanging emails and engaging in unstructured conversations to set the boundaries of the text. At a later stage, we had two long semi-structured conversations to capture and clarify our analytical points and methodological arguments. The second conversation was recorded, parts of it then being transcribed and edited for clarity and flow. The dialogue between us that is included in this chapter comes from this material. The remaining quotes are not verbatim but based on fieldnotes and memory.

In what follows, we will present some parts of our conversation on care and caring practices in research. We have each chosen to focus on a specific moment we have experienced with our research participants. While we retell those specific moments, we alternate between segments from our fieldwork notes, memories and dialogue. We then consider those moments by addressing possible causes that might have influenced us and engendered the discomfort. In the remaining section of the chapter, we reflect on what we have learned from those moments and how caring encounters affected our research relations and outcomes. By doing so, we also address some of the challenges and contradictions that may emerge from the social and emotional closeness between researcher and research participants. We conclude by offering some ideas on how to practise care as a method between researcher, research participant and the reader.

Caring dialogues

During one of our conversations, Eda recalled an illuminating moment in the field-work she conducted with Iranian queer refugees in Turkey. It took place after sev-eral fieldwork visits, which had begun around six months earlier. It also occurred at the very time Eda started to feel that some degree of rapport and trust between her and the (potential) research participants might have been built. She had some reasons to feel this way. For instance, more people had become willing to participate in the research. Also, the number of invitations that she received from the partici-pants to join in their everyday activities had been increasing. As well as that, a few households, which had a guest room or a couch to offer, had kindly and generously suggested that it may be time for Eda to check out of the hostel she used to stay in during her previous fieldwork visits. Besides, Eda was now feeling more at 'home' – or less out of place – at community events such as birthday parties, picnics or casual house gatherings. It was at one of those events that Kaveh[3], a cheerful, witty and straightforward research participant, criticized Eda for being distant and secretive, and invited her to be more sincere in the ongoing fieldwork relations. Eda reported Kaveh's comment in her fieldwork notes:

> Eda, it was always you who listened to our stories. You know our problems and griefs, but we don't know your story. Don't you have any trouble, pain or distress? Now it is your turn to tell.

In the earlier phases of the fieldwork, Eda had been asked about her educational background, her motivation for and relation to the research topic, her opinion on a particular matter, her migration to and life in Sweden and, to a lesser extent, about her political convictions, sexual orientation and her love life. Eda had believed that she had responded to those questions in a sincere way. Her answers, however, must have included only rarely – if they did at all – references to difficulties, weaknesses, confusions, problems, doubts, guilt, anxieties or vulnerabilities in her past and pres-ent. Otherwise, why would Kaveh ask her about her troubles, pain and distress?

Indeed, at the time Kaveh asked her this question, Eda was going through a difficult phase of life because of her mother's chronic illness. Eda's mother had long been living with cardiac insufficiency, an irremediable harm which had been caused by the inaccessibility of medicine to (proletarized) peasants in Turkey in the 1960s. Moreover, her medical condition had taken a turn for the worse soon after Eda began her doctoral studies in Sweden. Doctors started to say implicitly and explicitly that her mother's illness had reached a terminal stage. There was not much left to do except try to increase her life quality for the remaining time, whether it be a few months or a few years.

This is also what Eda disclosed in response to Kaveh's question, which was posed while they and some other research participants were having tea on a beautiful summer evening in one of the Anatolian cities where the Turkish state stipulates that international refugee applicants must reside throughout the time they wait in Turkey. With some tears in her eyes, Eda also talked about how *ghorbat/gurbet*[4] – referring to times she needed to be in Sweden – was making things more difficult for both her and her mother, who was at the time living alone in Ankara. Meanwhile, talking about the difficulties of absence from 'home' while having the privilege of being able to return to a 'home country' made Eda feel discomfort. After all, for other people at their table, it would be impossible or would cost a lot (ranging from jeopardizing their safety to losing their international protection status) to return to Iran or another country in case they wanted to spend some time with, take care of or say one last goodbye to someone they loved. Also, some of them had already told Eda that they had to leave their loved ones behind without knowing when they would see them again.

Eda therefore thought that she should recognize her privilege in terms of spatial mobility. Shading out her discomfort from her voice, Eda added in reply to Kaveh's question: 'But, of course, I can always come to Turkey to be with her during hospitalization periods or in case of emergency.' It was Mehran who kindly reacted to Eda's 'but' with something like this: 'Everyone has a problem, Eda. We cannot compare our problems. It is better to share them with each other, like our happiness.'

This is how Eda's fieldwork notes from that evening end. Although in those notes Eda did not mention how she and others in the group responded to Mehran's reminder, the critical exchange that took place on that summer evening and its emotional content had a transformative effect on Eda's emergent understanding of research relationships in connection with differences, commonalities, subjectivities, solidarity and caring.

⁊ ⊂ ʟ

EDA: I was like, 'wow, actually, I know this from political labour, but when it comes to research' – which is indeed political labour too, but… Anyway, I realized how, even though I was informed of critical methodologies that instruct us not to do so, I was marginalizing them, reproducing hegemonic images of [refugees]… Like, as if 'they are the most oppressed among oppressed, and I cannot compete with them when it comes to suffering'. The rest of the fieldwork, however, proved that it was me who needed help. I needed care, I needed support. I was supported. I am so thankful that they made this so clear at the very beginning. In the rest of the fieldwork, I was more *careful*, actually. More sharing as well.

POURAN: I think there are some valuable moments that are worth sharing here. Not just because we will write a text about it, but also for sharing with other people, because it's a circle. Like the more we get this information about forms of caring, about sharing and your pain, how to grieve and how to come out of it, then it will become easier also – I mean, for ourselves but also for other people. Then it will also not be unspoken and as a private area which is constantly there but is dealt with as something private we should not talk about.

EDA: Exactly.

POURAN: But I think also there's a value in sharing these moments of... I mean, when your research participant makes you [think about it], [it] gives you an 'aha' moment, a revelation about like, 'Oh wait, why am I not acknowledging my suffering? Why am I pushing it away?' Because it's also you're pushing yourself away from them, right?

EDA: Yeah, right.

POURAN: By saying, 'you're suffering much more than me: I am more privileged; you are damaged' I mean, 'suffering', we can never come close.

EDA: Yeah. And you reduce everything to just one thing like citizenship status, as if it is the only difference between us or... as if there are no commonalities between us.

POURAN: Your story reminds me...

> ʌ <

A couple of years ago, Pouran was going through a depression due to a life crisis. At the time, she was a full-time PhD student and had just started doing fieldwork. Parallel to her work she was engaged in the migrant rights movement, mainly in Malmö, which involved giving support to unaccompanied persons for housing, applying for economic aid, writing, reading and translating various documents, etc. During a period of her fieldwork she shared a flat with a young person who was living undocumented and waiting to seek asylum anew, and who later also became one of the research participants of her study. They shared several other parts of their lives together too and, as they could communicate through the same mother tongue, a certain intimacy was established between them. Mostly, however, the relationship was formed by Pouran taking on a self-imposed supportive role.

POURAN: And then when I was in this depression, I don't even remember how the conversation started because I was used to being the one supporting them, hugging them or patting their back when they were having anxiety attacks or whatever. So I wasn't used to opening up.

But during that time, she did open up and started sharing how she was feeling unwell and did not feel motivated at all. She used to wake up and feel an intense burden of having to get through the day, wanting the day to end so that she could go back to sleep and be unbothered. As she was sharing these intimate and painful feelings, her flatmate affirmed her experience, saying that this was exactly how they felt every day. The anxiety of living undocumented had transformed them into this depressive person, which, according to them, had become their normal state of being. By Pouran opening up to her flatmate, something shifted in their relationship.

POURAN: And I would never have understood them if I had never opened up and told them about where I am. And, you know, that also changed something in our relationship. They were giving me support, they were also telling me, 'I feel you, I understand you.' My suffering wasn't, of course, [to be] compared to theirs. But in the interaction we had, they said: 'Yeah, I feel a very similar feeling.'

This intimate moment of connection that took place was nothing that Pouran had anticipated. The difference in their citizenship status had permeated the very foundation of their relationship. They could talk and get close in the sense that they would speak in their mother tongue, but this closeness was never in depth and reciprocal. This was mainly the result of Pouran's perception that the difference between them was greater than the commonalities they shared. After all, her flatmate was in such an existential crisis – the prevailing risk that the police could find them and deport them from Sweden, or that they would have to wait even longer with the risk of again being denied residency. This uncertainty pervaded their everyday life, along with having been separated from their home and family, and not knowing when or if they would ever be able to reunite. Pouran's privileged position of having residency, and her family being quite close and financially comfortable, made her in a way situate herself 'above' her flatmate, which hindered her from seeing how they could communicate on an equal level.

POURAN: Yeah, when I realized that, I also felt embarrassed. I remember how that was a strong feeling I'd had until then, thinking that we couldn't be close. And that I was surprised that we had a connection. It was really one of those moments – you know… lessons, life lessons I carry with me.

Reciprocities of care

What is common to our stories is that they illustrate the methodological, ethico-political and personal value of 'revelatory moments' (Trigger, Forsey and Meurk 2012) and caring encounters in research. To begin with, the moments and exchanges we describe above enabled us to *practise reflexivity* in the research process, instead of *being reflexive* only in the writing process (Skeggs 2002). A reflexive research process, as Sultana puts it, 'can be a transformative process whereby the researcher is not only aware of but accounts for power relations, changing subjectivities, and overall effects over time and space' (2017, p. 1).

The revelatory moments we experienced early in our doctoral research process revealed immediately the social and emotional distance we had imposed between us and our research participants. This was unexpected for both of us because, when these moments took place, we had perceived ourselves as caring, warm, understanding and respectful researchers. While some other research participants may have perceived us in that way too, these moments confirmed the well-known methodological fact that the position of the ethnographer vis-à-vis the research participants is dependent not only on how they perceive themselves 'but also how participants respond to and perceive them – which can include many different experiences even within a single community or field site' (Davis and Craven 2016, p. 60). Facing the self-imposed distance between us and our participants was stunning also because we, novice ethnographers informed by critical methodologies, had been striving to dissociate ourselves from positivist notions of detachment by 'rejecting the separations between subject and object, thought and feeling, knower and known, and political and personal' (Stacey 1988, p. 21). Therefore, the tacit invitation we received to review how we relate to people with whom we work was timely and crucial.

Not to diminish the importance of the work of researchers who argue for closeness in social science research (Hill Collins 1986, Behar 1996, Anzaldúa 2012, Back 2012), the legacy of maintaining a boundary-like separation between researcher and research field is, however, still intact in traditional academic disciplines. Our stories illustrate that it may take time to unlearn these powerful logics and to practise critical methodologies. 'I remember [...] thinking that we couldn't be close,' as Pouran puts it, is a striking example in this regard. Her starting point from the outset, with inspiration from her activism of helping and giving support to others, had been to enable closeness in her fieldwork towards the research participants. But allowing the research participants to come close to *her* had not occurred to her as equally relevant. Similarly, Eda, herself a young migrant woman and a minoritized doctoral researcher in a Western European context, felt discomfort while disclosing her sorrow and suffering across borders because of her privilege of mobility between Sweden and Turkey. Her discomfort not only distanced her from people she worked with but also pushed her to de-emphasize her suffering and sorrow. As a result, she overlooked what they (she and her research participants) had in common: empathy, care and the precariousness of migranthood to which each of them was exposed differentially vis-à-vis the multiple and intersecting power relations within and across migrant groups.

Reflexivity requires us not only to account for our positionalities but also to recognize that 'all knowledge is the product of specific relations in specific times and places, and that specificity is part of the essence of understanding and making sense of research' (Jones *et al.* 2017, p. 117). The critical exchange in our stories directed us to the question: Would we act, think, feel in the same way if we had worked with a non-migrant social group or, more importantly, with another group of migrants, say so-called highly skilled migrant workers or lifestyle migrants? Might it be the case that we had internalized some of the main pillars of the migration and border regimes, such as: the radical dichotomy between 'us and them', and the internal hierarchies within those regimes as reflected in myriad distinctions 'imposed by the state and general public on migrants' (Luibhéid 2005, p. xi)?

Caring relationships pervade all kinds of research, although it is usually caring performances of researchers that are addressed, recognized, problematized or even celebrated in research accounts and narratives (Toombs *et al.* 2016). The unidirectional perception of care contains a risk of othering and patronizing research participants, and this risk can be stronger in research settings that are hegemonically associated with service-oriented notions of care, such as research on homelessness, or humanitarian or disability studies (ibid.). We argue that the hegemonic images of refugees and asylum-seeking migrants as 'powerless', 'vulnerable', 'desperate', and 'undifferentiated subjects of international humanitarian assistance' (Said 2001, Bauman 2002), along with migration research which is still too often influenced by a psychological understanding (Andersson *et al.* 2010, Eide 2012, Ascher 2014), could have influenced our perspective and performances of care. Being used to seeing the asylum-seeking migrant subject foremost as 'in need of care', it did not occur to us that we were transferring this stereotype during our encounters with our research participants. Pouran's story exemplifies this by her being accustomed to 'being the one supporting them, hugging them or patting their back'. It had not dawned on her that she could also be cared for by her flatmate and that her pain could be worth sharing. From this very important revelation, Pouran's view towards and relationship with her research participants gradually shifted. Periods of feeling sad or unwell were met by text messages of encouragement and home-cooked meals being delivered to her home. Her parents, brother and friends started developing their own relationships with the research participants as a result of sharing intimate moments such as birthdays and holiday festivities. Pouran also started feeling comfortable about sharing her (family's) post-migratory life story of growing up in a suburban area in Stockholm, Sweden, during the 1980s and 1990s, with the hopes and sorrows of her parents' and family's struggles in the failed Iranian revolution that overshadowed her childhood, and the sense of betweenship[5] (Jagne-Soreau 2019) that had developed through complexities of intergenerational diasporic lived experiences along with her identity of Swedishness.

Eda's research progressed in parallel with the deterioration of her mother's health. This marked later stages of fieldwork with deep sorrow, anger at the structural factors that had worsened her mother's illness, self-reproach for not managing to be a 'good' caregiver across borders while amidst the anxieties of being a doctoral student, and the accompanying ripple of guilt for not doing justice to her PhD studies at the times when she needed to give transnational care, as well as waiting for the devastating loss of her mother to happen. Yet, these were also times that were pleasantly marked by, among other things, small victories against illness, moments of wellness, the joy of becoming a teacher and researcher, and the caring relationships that emanated from the research. Caring relationships in her research not only enabled Eda to better reflect on differences and commonalities in terms of the multiple and shifting positionings and diasporic experiences in the field (see also Naldemirci 2013, pp. 53–56), but also eased her affective struggles embedded in (transnational) care work. A few examples of this occurred when she had to interrupt the fieldwork upon a telephone call letting her know that her mother had been hospitalized or that Eda needed to stay in Ankara longer than planned when she came to Turkey to conduct fieldwork. In such moments, research participants around her provided Eda with various acts of care such as checking in on her regularly, sending best wishes (or prayers if they were spiritually minded), and sharing their similar experiences of caring for a beloved one, illness or grief.

Caring relationships also enabled Eda to invite her research participants to her mother's home at times when they were in Ankara to complete a bureaucratic procedure regarding their asylum applications. Not all of them could, or wanted, to come. Some preferred to meet outside. A few came for a short visit to have tea or lunch together, while a few others stayed for 1 or 2 days, either alone or with a partner, or with a family member visiting from Iran. Those visits generated close (and sometimes complex) encounters across multiple subjectivities and axes of power such as generation, class, sexuality, gender, culture and citizenship. Before those encounters, class mobilities and temporary fluctuations in class positions of the research participants because of their queer displacement were visible to Eda, the researcher, but her own upward mobility through education became (more) visible to the research participants once they visited the house where Eda's mother used to live – an old, semi-detached house in a working-/lower-middle-class suburb of Ankara – and met her mother, a divorced woman in her late 50s, a public worker with a high school degree who had retired early due to chronic illness, a mystic and practising Muslim who was just one generation away from her rural roots. This and similar encounters brought the researcher and research participants closer, and it also meant that they perceived the relation between them in a more egalitarian way. Analytically, it would require another text to do justice to those encounters. Meanwhile, Eda was not fully aware of their sociological importance and political value until her mother passed away. For instance, it was only after her mother died that Eda came to learn that her mother and one of the research participants, who had visited the home in Ankara, had been developing a caring relationship across borders (both literal and metaphorical) and beyond this research.

The moments shared above taught us to listen more closely (Back 2007), to engage with our research participants (Jones *et al.* 2017) and to see the significance in sharing care as a mutual practice (Harris and Fortney 2017). When research participants questioned why we stayed distant, they indicated that they felt close enough to us to care about our distance. When they invited us to 'come closer' in those specific moments, they also invited us to see and treat them 'as active co-producers of knowledge' (Giametta 2018, p. 874). For this very reason, we find it important to recognize the methodological issues, challenges and contradictions that may arise from close engagement in research relationships.

Writing about caring encounters and relationships might carry the risk of romanticizing and universalizing a common experience of care in the field (Naldemirci 2013, pp. 53–56). However, the multiple, complex and shifting positionings of research subjects (researcher and research participants) make it impossible to stand at an equal distance (or closeness) to every person in the social and emotional field. Of course, not every research participant invited us to 'come closer'. A few even made it clear, often indirectly, that they would like to limit their research participation to an interview or to the fieldwork process of research. What we have learned from such research interactions is that the researcher has the responsibility to *carefully* observe 'the signals' in the field. Furthermore, we are informed by our and other researchers' post-fieldwork experiences that multiple precarities of life, the gendered, classed and ableist pressures of neoliberal academia, which 'requires high productivity in compressed time frames' (Mountz et al. 2015), and some other un/predictable factors may prevent both the researcher and the research participants from nourishing or maintaining caring relationships that they formed during the research, and yield to feelings of disappointment, abandonment, discomfort and guilt (see Huisman 2008).

In qualitative research, particularly in long-term ethnographies like ours, the employment of critical research principles such as rapport, empathy, political intimacy and reciprocity may blur the boundaries between 'research relations' and 'personal relations' (see, among others, Stacey 1988, Acker *et al.* 1991, Patai 1991, Huisman 2008, Gajparia 2017). This may easily result in unintentional or undesirable disclosures and revelations from both sides of the research relationship. Unlike the research participant, however, the researcher can perceive and record the entire experience as data (Ramazanoglu and Holland 2002, p.158). Therefore, there always exists the danger of manipulating closeness in the field for the aim of gathering data (Acker *et al.* 1991, p. 141). Furthermore, what still remains dominant in research is 'the power of researchers to interpret their selection of data through their own ideas and values, and in terms of their chosen epistemology' (Ramazanoglu and Holland 2002, p. 115). All research involves ethical challenges, problems and contradictions of various kinds, and our ethnographies are no exception. Yet we, informed by critical methodologies, believe that 'there is value in working through the messiness, engaging in fieldwork in a *careful* manner, rather than writing it off as too fraught with difficulties and dangers' (Hyndman 2001, p. 265, *emphasis added*). While it would require another chapter to properly discuss the ethical issues that emerged in our ethnographies, we would like to underline that 'in an unethical world, we cannot do truly ethical research' (Patai 1991, p. 150). What we can do is 'to make up our minds whether our research is worth doing or not, and then' proceed with critical research principles (ibid.). We can, for instance, begin by recognizing vulnerability embedded in 'our interpersonal bonds to others', and remind ourselves to be attentive to 'the reality and practice of changing relationships with our research participants over time' (Ellis 2007, p. 4). Moreover, what is pivotal is to question and reflect on our ethical choices in each step of the research, not only before and during the fieldwork, but even after the research is done (Huisman 2008). This would mean that we, researchers and research communities, should spend more time on pondering how to write 'in a way that is intellectually honest and politically responsible', and such as to 'humanize but not to romanticize or idealize' (Ghannam 2013, p. 26). Despite all these precautions, we may fail again. And to mitigate the risk of failing again or to 'fail better' we need to unlearn hiding our failures from each other, from ourselves (Clark and Sousa 2020, p.2), and from our research participants. On the other hand, we, standing on the hierarchical ladders of the university, are aware that only a few 'are in a position to admit and explore failure as an academic project' (Bliesemann de Guevara and Kurowska 2020, p. 170). What we have learned from the Collective and our dialogue is that our failures, when shared *care-fully*, have the potential to erode academic hierarchies and myths (see also Clark and Sousa 2020). Our stories have taught us not to be caught up in navel-gazing and that we can and need to be kind to ourselves and towards our research (Mountz *et al.* 2015). This is also what we were told by some of our research participants during and after fieldwork. Which brings us to the very heart of the analysis in this chapter – namely, the question of care and caring practices in research.

Caring is sharing

We take inspiration from Tronto's post-human definition of care as a 'species activity that includes everything we do to maintain, contain, and repair our 'world' so that we can live in it as well as possible' (1993, p. 103). This notion of care connects to an understanding that care is associated with the concept of burden. To care is to carry the burden for another human or species. It is essentially a matter of empathy (Collins 1989). And this is also where our understanding of caring is rooted: that there needs to be an underlying capacity to identify with someone or something else. To care, in this understanding, can never be a one-way practice, as Harris and Fortney (2017) so distinctly put it, as it involves reciprocal engagement and imagining from the other's perspective.

The examples given above illustrate how our own caring practices leading up to the revelatory moments were broken, in the sense that we had not been able to imagine ourselves as being the subject of care (by the research participants). We had been mostly interested in how we could care for the participants, and we failed to do it in an egalitarian way. Our reflexive repetition had been centred on critical reading and thinking about our differences and the issue of representation, without giving any deep consideration to what it is that *connects* us as researcher and research participants. Such a reflexive starting point, where the researcher is focused mainly on a self-centred practice that essentially has little linking to others, produces a disconnection from 'mutual, willful vulnerability' (Harris and Fortney 2017, p. 22). By overturning this order, the reflexive practice can instead be an interactive process and exchange, resulting in a 'reflexive caring' that has the capacity to fundamentally change relationships.

> Reflexive caring connects to many aspects of performance: enacting mundane interpersonal encounters, building relationships with research participants, mentoring students and junior colleagues, crafting personal narrative and performative writing, encouraging authors and conference goers to revise their thinking, inviting a relational and posthuman turn.
>
> (2017, pp. 20 f.)

Harris and Fortney not only capture the need for reflexive caring between researcher, research participant, students and colleagues but also argue that their understanding of reflexive caring involves the relation between writer and reader too. Seeing that the reader at times agrees and many times disagrees, wants something different from a text, asks for clarity or requests fluidity, the process of reflexive practice that this calls forth requires that the practice of caring is under constant revision. Without neglecting the importance of how our different subject positions affect who can open up to whom, whose words are heard and whose ears are deemed important to speak to, we sympathize with this understanding of conceptualizing reflexive caring as it allows for our shifting positionalities to be acknowledged along with the need for a reciprocity of affectionate relations with 'others'.

A final point that we wish to stress here, inspired by Harris and Fortney (2017), is the consequence of sharing, vis-à-vis our emotions with our research participants and our insights presented to you, the reader. We see this as an interconnected practice of caring as it allows for closeness *as well as* a knowledge transfer. *Sharing is caring*, as the well-quoted phrase says. We found ourselves able to share our stories with our research participants because they cared for us and allowed for a supportive environment for us to feel safe, which was intertwined with our care and engagement in *their* stories and lives. Accordingly, we would like to turn around the expression to highlight the reciprocity in caring practices, namely that *caring is sharing*. To say that you care for someone involves the act of letting someone into your personal space. Along these lines, we see this chapter as an attempt to reveal ourselves to you, the reader, through this caring practice.

Notes

1 Following the conceptualization by MacDonald, we use the term 'encounter' to refer to 'the multiple and fragmented ways' in which 'subjects are called not only into being in relationship with one another, but also in relationship to history, geography and a myriad of other constellations' (2020, p. 252).

2 The Turkish state still maintains the geographical limitation to the 1951 Refugee Convention. International refugee applicants coming from outside 'Europe' are permitted to stay in the country until their legal status is determined and the UN Refugee Agency finds a 'durable' solution, which usually means 'resettlement to a third country'. At the time of Eda's research, the third countries that accepted Iranian LGBT refugees who received their legal status in Turkey were Canada, the United States and, to a lesser extent, Australia, and the average waiting time was around two to three years.

3 All identifying details have been anonymized.

4 A common word in Persian and Turkish, originally from Arabic, that can roughly be translated as '[being in] a foreign land, or absence from home'.

5 The term derives from the Swedish word and notion *mellanförskap*, which comprises the experience of mixed-race adoptees and children of immigrants who neither feel fully at home in an imagined 'homeland' nor in Swedish society. Thus a 'betweenship' captures both the position of being neither–nor and at the same time a mixed/hybrid identity. Similarly, Homi Bhabha (1994) conceptualizes experiences of in-betweenness.

References

Acker, J. et al., 1991. Objectivity and truth: Problems in doing feminist resarch. In: M.M. Fonow and J.A. Cook, eds. *Beyond Methodology: Feminist Scholarship as Lived Research.* Bloomington, IN: Indiana University Press.

Andersson, H.E. et al., 2010. *Mellan det förflutna och framtiden: Asylsökande barns välfärd, hälsa och välbefinnande [Between the past and the future: Asylum-seeking children's welfare, health and well-being].* Centrum för Europaforskning, Göteborg: Göteborgs universitet (CERGU).

Anzaldúa, G., 2012[1987]. *Borderlands/La Frontera: The New Mestiza.* San Francisco: Aunt Lute Books.

Ascher, H., 2014. From apathy to activity: Experiences of refugee children with severe withdrawal syndrome. In: G. Overland, E. Guribye and B. Lie, eds. *Nordic Work with Traumatised Refugees: Do We Really Care.* Newcastle: Cambridge Scholars.

Back, L., 2007. *The Art of Listening.* Oxford; New York: Berg.

Back, L., 2012. Live sociology: Social research and its futures. *Sociological Review,* 60 (1), 18–39. doi:10.1111/j.1467-954X.2012.02115.x.

Bauman, Z., 2002. In the lowly nowherevilles of liquid modernity: Comments on and around Agier. *Ethnography,* 3 (3), 343–349.

Behar, R., 1996. *The Vulnerable Observer: Anthropology That Breaks Your Heart.* Boston: Beacon Press.

Bhabha, H.K., 1994. *The Location of Culture.* London: Routledge.

Bliesemann de Guevara, B. and Kurowska, X., 2020. Building on ruins or patching up the possible? Reinscribing fieldwork failure in IR as a productive rupture. In: K. Kušić and J. Záhora, eds. *Fieldwork as Failure: Living and Knowing in the Field of International Relations.* Bristol: E-International Relations.

Clark, A.M. and Sousa, B.J., 2020. A manifesto for better research failure. *International Journal of Qualitative Methods,* 19 (1–3). doi:10.1177/1609406920973858.

Collins, P.H., 1989. The social construction of Black feminist thought. *Signs,* 14 (4), 745–773.

Davis, D.-A. and Craven, C., 2016. *Feminist Ethnography: Thinking through Methodologies, Challenges, and Possibilities.* Lanham: Rowman & Littlefield.

Djampour, P., 2018. *Borders Crossing Bodies: The Stories of Eight Youth with Experience of Migrating.* Thesis (PhD). Malmö: Malmö University.

Eide, K., 2012. *Barn på flukt: Psykososialt arbeid med enslige mindreårige flyktninger [Children in Flight: Psychosocial Work with Unaccompanied Underage Refugees].* Oslo: Gyldendal Akademisk.

Ellis, C., 2007. Telling secrets, revealing lives: Relational ethics in research with intimate others. *Qualitative Inquiry,* 13 (1), 3–29. doi:10.1177/1077800406294947.

Gajparia, J., 2017. Capitalising on rapport, emotional labour and colluding with the neoliberal academy. *Women's Studies International Forum,* 61, 87–92. doi:10.1016/j.wsif.2016.10.015.

Ghannam, F., 2013. *Live and Die Like a Man: Gender Dynamics in Urban Egypt.* Stanford, CA: Stanford University Press.

Giametta, C., 2018. Reorienting participation, distance and positionality: Ethnographic encounters with gender and sexual minority migrants. *Sexualities,* 21 (5), 868–882. doi:10.1177/1363460716678751.

Harris, K.L. and Fortney, J.M., 2017. Performing reflexive caring: Rethinking reflexivity through trauma and disability. *Text and Performance Quarterly,* 37 (1), 20–34. doi:10.1080/10462937.2016.1273543.

Hill Collins, P., 1986. Learning from the outsider within: The sociological significance of Black feminist thought. *Social Problems,* 33 (6), S14–S32. doi:10.1525/sp.1986.33.6.03a00020.

Huisman, K., 2008. 'Does this mean you`re not going to come visit me anymore?': An inquiry into an ethics of reciprocity and positionality in feminist research. *Sociological Inquiry*, 78 (3), 372–396. doi:10.1111/j.1475-682X.2008.00244.x.

Hyndman, J., 2001. The field as here and now, not there and then. *Geographical Review*, 91 (1/2), 262–272. doi:10.2307/3250827.

Jagne-Soreau, M., 2019. Att vakna upp som suedi: Om mellanförskap och rap [Waking up as a Swede: On intercourse and rap]. *Nordisk poesi: Tidsskrift for lyrikkforskning*, 4 (1), 43–60.

Jones, H. et al., 2017. *Go home? The politics of immigration controversies*. Manchester: Manchester University Press. doi:10.7765/9781526117946.

Luibhéid, E., 2005. Introduction: Queering migration and citizenship. In: E. Luibhéid and L. Cantú, Jr., eds. *Queer Migrations. Sexuality, U.S. Citizenship, and Border Crossings*. Minneapolis, MN: University of Minnesota Press, ix–xlvi.

Lundberg, A. and Farahani, F., 2017. I dialog: Intersektionella läsningar av hemhörighet, migration och kunskapsproduktion [In dialogue: Intersectional readings of belonging, migration and knowledge production]. *Tidskrift för genusvetenskap*, 38 (3), 77–101.

MacDonald, K., 2020. Toward a transnational feminist methodology of encounter. *Qualitative Research*, 20 (3), 249–264. doi:10.1177/1468794119847578.

Mountz, A. et al., 2015. For slow scholarship: A feminist politics of resistance through collective action in the neoliberal university. *Acme: An International E-Journal for Critical Geographies*, 14 (4), 1235–1259.

Naldemirci, Ö., 2013. *Caring (in) Diaspora: Aging and Caring Experiences of Older Turkish Migrants in a Swedish Context*. Thesis (PhD). Gothenburg: University of Gothenburg.

Patai, D., 1991. U.S. Academics and third world women: Is ethical research possible? In: S.B. Gluck and D. Patai, eds. *Women's Words: Feminist Practice of Oral History*. New York: Routledge.

Ramazanoglu, C. and Holland, J., 2002. *Feminist Methodology: Challenges and Choices* London: SAGE, 115.

Said, E.W., 2001. Reflections on Exile. In: *Reflections on Exile and Other Essays*. London: Granta Books.

Skeggs, B., 2002. Techniques for telling the reflexive self. In: T. May, ed. *Qualitative Research in Action*. London: SAGE, 349–374.

Stacey, J., 1988. Can there be a feminist ethnography? *Women's Studies International Forum*, 11 (1), 21–27.

Sultana, F., 2017. Reflexivity. *International Encyclopedia of Geography: People, the Earth, Environment and Technology*, 1–5. doi:10.1017/UPO9781844654031.017.

Toombs, A. et al., 2016. From empathy to care: A feminist care ethics perspective on long-term researcher-participant relations. *Interacting with Computers*, 29 (1), 45–57. doi:10.1093/iwc/iww010.

Trigger, D., Forsey, M. and Meurk, C., 2012. Revelatory moments in fieldwork. *Qualitative Research*, 12 (5), 513 –527. doi:10.1177/1468794112446049.

Tronto, J.C., 1993. *Moral Boundaries: A Political Argument for an Ethic of Care*. New York: Routledge.

AFTERWORD

Diana Mulinari

How research is conducted, who is involved, on which terms and, most importantly, who benefits from research results have been at the core of feminist scholarship since its establishment as an academic discipline. Who can be a knower and what can be known frame issues of representation and intersubjectivity at centre stage in feminist epistemological and methodological debates, inspiring and shaping feminist developments in the field of qualitative methodologies.

The Politics and Ethics of Representation in Qualitative Research: Addressing Moments of Discomfort engages in these and similar questions, expanding the tradition through conceptualizing moments of discomfort as sites of knowledge production for reflecting on the politics and ethics of the qualitative research process. Contributors approach the subject from different perspectives, critically examining their quite diverse social identities in naming the joy and the pain in the everyday doing of qualitative methods and in exploring the tensions between academic knowledge production and practices of solidarity and care. The contributors enter into a dialogue with both their research subjects and the reader in a way that is courageous, passionate and analytically powerful. The texts written by *The Critical Methodologies Collective* are crafted through the efforts and the dilemmas of thinking together, challenging neoliberal agendas that encourage division and competition, and exploring practices and strategies of building nurturing academic communities committed to diverse forms of gender and sexual justice(s).

Needless to say, methodological and ethical dilemmas become acute in the context of a number of societal transformations in Europe generally and in Sweden more specifically, where most contributors to the anthology are located. Sweden, for many decades a role model of societal inclusion, gender equality and human rights, is today located at the crossroads of, on the one hand, neoliberal discourses of austerity played out through soaring racialized and gendered inequalities and, on the other, exclusionary racist discourses on the threat of migration (and migrants) to the welfare state, in a context of the success of ethnonationalist political parties and a growing visibility of anti-genderism in public debates.

These societal transformations (resisted and challenged by a variety of social movements and solidarity networks) create a number of radical demands on feminist methodologies, and generate sharp dilemmas, making critical reflections on methodological journeys extremely needed while also more challenging than ever.

The anthology is a powerful contribution to the scholarly work challenging epistemologies of ignorance and epistemic injustices. It takes as a point of departure the fundamental role of listening and learning with and through others, particularly from others whose experiences, and meanings (of heteronormativity, colonialism and diverse forms of racism), become invisible, unnoticed, concealed, or simply – and violently – excluded within mainstream academia.

Inventing, developing and exploring methodological strategies (and sometimes failing in doing so) is at the core of this scholarly work that provides cautious, careful and reflective explorations of the embodied experience, of the 'doing qualitative methods' in the everyday of both the researcher and the researched. Challenging the tendency within the qualitative tradition towards forms of authoritative arrogance shaped by the (racist) desire to know the other, the volume recuperates humanness and emphasizes the difficult labour of interconnection and intersubjectivity that is constitutive of feminist qualitative methods.

The labour of care is at its best when acknowledging the shortcomings of methodological frames and methods of 'giving voice' or mediating 'the view from below', asserting meanwhile that an exploration of the political economy of location and representation, although essential to feminist qualitative methodologies, is not sufficient.

Scholars in the volume identify and explore a number of dilemmas in the ways through which boundaries are transgressed in their own research practices: between work and personal life, between academic work and political engagement, and between intimacy and des-identification with research subjects. The different chapters share the efforts, the failures, but also the productive strategies evolving from boundary-transgressing, with an emphasis on practices of accountability and responsibility towards research subjects and the research community.

Vulnerability is a relevant topic of the analysis through the anthology: the vulnerability of the researcher as well as of the researched, courageously exploring the nature of vulnerability (or, rather, the tensions between experienced vulnerability and the researchers' diverse privileged locations and social identities); but also the responsibilities owed to vulnerable research subjects, with special focus on who bears these responsibilities.

This scholarly work holds immense promise for feminist and critical scholarship. It shares important methodological knowledge without providing a method handbook, holding onto hope regarding the relevance of feminist qualitative traditions without falling into either pessimistic readings or romantic agendas, and shifting experiences of vulnerability and discomfort from auto-referential agendas towards the creation of epistemic feminist communities of struggle.

A beautifully written, sensible, investigative and wise book that will be an excellent companion for times to come.

EPILOGUE

What the Collective has meant to us

The Critical Methodologies Collective

VANNA: This group has been a solidary space within academia, where we have been able to laugh, cry and develop our thoughts as well as reflect on our anxieties with support from others facing similar dilemmas and discomforts. Since my first year as a PhD student, this group has been very special to me. We have not only discussed our projects, but have shared ups and downs in writing and in life in general. Coming from different departments and research contexts, being unified by an interest in methodological dilemmas − and hence a feeling of discomfort when performing our studies − we have built a friendship that has made me feel more at home within academia.

PANKHURI: The Collective has been a space to move away from rigid notions of what constitutes academic engagement, to a freer space which allows for experimenting with different structures, tools and ways of thinking and writing. In doing so, one cannot always find, locate or measure progress but only sit with the range of discomforts being discussed and reflected upon. The Collective in this way is a rapture for the ruptures of intellectual gaps and thinking in academia. It is also a source of expanding my feminist consciousness; to find my experience in others' words in different intersectional, regional and cultural settings. To be a part of the Collective has therefore been like an act of resistance − to explore the full range of intellectual engagement (the ugly, uncomfortable and embarrassing and not just the successes, solutions or advancements) in our respective academic lives. The fact that this book was completed within set timelines even amidst a world pandemic, with the added constraints of care work and illnesses, is testament to the collective care and feminist solidarity that members have embodied and practised together.

MARTA: I remember when Vanna asked me, some ten years ago, if I would like to join the group. My first instinct was to reply, 'I don't think I will have time for this.' One of the things that the Collective has meant for me was to unlearn and resist this kind of notion of time, a notion that is so hegemonic in academia today. This has been not so much about *using* time in other ways, but about attempting to transform the very *terms* that define the ways in which time can be experienced.

KATRINE: The Collective has for me been a space for academic reflection outside of institutional settings and restraints. We have arranged workshops together, cooked and eaten lunches together, read each other's unfinished, vulnerable texts, and engaged in discussions again and again because we *chose* to. In the Collective, I have felt a belonging to an embodied version of academia where it has been possible to be whole people with both analytical and emotional responses to our work and the world in which this work takes place.

TOVE: When I think of the Collective, the word that comes to mind is 'space'. Space to think, space to learn, space to be unknowing and stupid, space to stay in discomfort without a feeling of needing to fix things, as well as a feeling of 'holding space'. I have seldom been in an academic context where I have felt as much support as I have in the Collective. Meanwhile, there have been times when everything said at a seminar, meeting or workshop has been unintelligible to me. I typically experience such situations as daunting. However, in the space provided in the Collective, such experiences of discomfort have helped me find new spaces in myself, in my thinking, in my learning, in theory as well as in academia.

EMMA: In an allowing setting, the Collective has provided a space for discussion, for learning from the ongoing work of others and for addressing difficult and painful aspects of my research. I must admit that our meetings sometimes caused anxiety, as the insights from the others triggered feelings of insufficiency in terms of my previous reading, knowledge, analytical skills, etc. Maybe the anxiety can be a sign that working collectively on themes connected to the politics and ethics of research, in particular addressing discomforts, can itself at times be a dis/comforting experience. Many times I think these themes are hidden in the 'final product' (in the case of a PhD, the thesis) and therefore not visible and/or theorized or learnt from. The main experience, however, of working together and of forming a collective is connected to feelings of pride and gratitude: I am proud of our work and of our Collective, and grateful to be a part of it.

JOHANNA: The Collective, to me, means not being alone in the otherwise often lonesome academic environment. For instance, while working on this volume it has meant sharing thoughts, texts and anxieties without feeling uncomfortable. It has also meant shared responsibility, in that there is always someone to cover for you or help out if aspects of one's personal life make work life difficult.

POURAN: I was introduced to the Collective at a stage in my doctoral studies when I felt insecure about what it was I was doing in academia and how I would pursue my research. The timing couldn't have been better, as this space of critical knowledge reciprocation and caring for each other would time and again remind me of why I wanted to finish my thesis and keep learning, keep sharing. To me, the Collective is still as important today as it was back then.

EDA HATICE: 'What the Collective means to me' is the title of the Word document I opened to add my response. The question reminds me of an inspiring quote from bell hooks' *Teaching to Transgress*. The quote concludes the book and reads as follows:

> The academy is not paradise. But learning is a place where paradise can be created. The classroom, with all its limitations, remains a location of possibility. In that field of possibility we have the opportunity to labor for freedom, to demand of ourselves and our comrades, an openness of mind and heart that allows us to face reality even as we collectively imagine ways to move beyond boundaries, to transgress. This is education as the practice of freedom.
>
> (hooks 1994, p. 207)

I love sharing this quote with the participants of classes and lectures I teach. Yet I had not read it in relation to our Collective before. Looking back on our almost-decade-long union to write this volume made me realize that I understand and experience the Collective as another 'location of possibility' in academia.

When I joined the Collective soon after I started my doctoral studies, it meant to me a supportive reading group where I read and thought about critical and emancipatory methodologies together with fellow graduate students. In time, however, both the Collective and my participation in the Collective took on a new meaning.

If you arrived in Western academia as a 'non-European' woman who is the first among her extended family ever to set foot in a 'foreign' land and to speak in a 'foreign' language, it is very likely that you would feel discomfort in classrooms, corridors, seminar rooms or conferences. The Collective has provided me with academic space in which I can talk about my discomfort in comfort.

I consider being a part of such a collective both a luxury and a necessity. Building and sustaining caring communities within academia is crucial, particularly for those academic workers and students whose thoughts, bodies, and lives do not conform to hegemonic norms and those who have caring needs and responsibilities beyond the normative/binary, ethnonationalist, neoliberal, and speciesist logics of welfare regimes.

The Collective has taken care of me. It has nurtured me, politically and intellectually. When I had to take a break from work, the Collective made sure that there would be someone at 'home' to open the door when I came back.

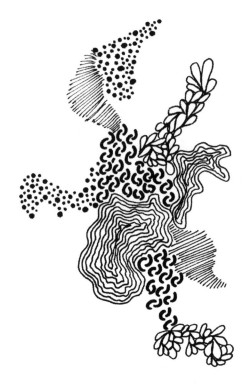

References

hooks, bell, 1994. *Teaching to Transgress: Education as the Practice of Freedom.* New York; London: Routledge.

INDEX

Page numbers followed by 'n' refer to notes numbers